Electronic Warfare

I0439991

U.S. Marine Corps

PCN 143 000104 00

DISTRIBUTION STATEMENT A: Approved for public; distribution is unlimited

To Our Readers

Changes: Readers of this publication are encouraged to submit suggestions and changes that will improve it. Recommendations may be sent directly to Commanding General, Marine Corps Combat Development Command, Doctrine Division (C 42), 3300 Russell Road, Suite 318A, Quantico, VA 22134-5021 or by fax to 703-784-2917 (DSN 278-2917) or by E-mail to **morgann@mccdc.usmc.mil**. Recommendations should include the following information:

- Location of change
  Publication number and title
  Current page number
  Paragraph number (if applicable)
  Line number
  Figure or table number (if applicable)
- Nature of change
  Add, delete
  Proposed new text, preferably double-spaced and typewritten
- Justification and/or source of change

Additional copies: A printed copy of this publication may be obtained from Marine Corps Logistics Base, Albany, GA 31704-5001, by following the instructions in MCBul 5600, *Marine Corps Doctrinal Publications Status.* An electronic copy may be obtained from the Doctrine Division, MCCDC, world wide web home page which is found at the following universal reference locator: **http://www.doctrine.usmc.mil**.

DEPARTMENT OF THE NAVY
Headquarters United States Marine Corps
Washington, D.C. 20380-1775

10 September 2002

FOREWORD

Marine Corps Warfighting Publication (MCWP) 3-40.5, *Electronic Warfare*, provides doctrine for the employment and use of electronic warfare in support of the Marine air-ground task force (MAGTF). Electronic warfare doctrine provides a basis for—

- Effective integration of electronic warfare within the MAGTF.
- Coordination and cooperation with joint force components, particularly for the effective employment of electronic warfare resources.
- Operational, procedural, and technical interoperability at the operational and tactical level.
- The exchange of electronic warfare information and intelligence between United States forces and allied nations or multinational partners.

This publication provides an overview of electronic warfare doctrine and tasks. It also discusses electronic warfare structure within MAGTF, joint, and multinational operations. This publication is intended for any Marine involved in the planning and execution of electronic warfare operations.

MCWP 3-40.5 supersedes Fleet Marine Force Manual (FMFM) 7-12, *Electronic Warfare*, dated 20 May 1991.

Reviewed and approved this date.

BY DIRECTION OF THE COMMANDANT OF THE MARINE CORPS

EDWARD HANLON, JR.
Lieutenant General, U.S. Marine Corps
Commanding General
Marine Corps Combat Development Command
Quantico, Virginia

Publication Control Number: 143 000104 00

Electronic Warfare

Table of Contents

Chapter 4. Joint and Multinational Operations

Chapter 5. MAGTF Electronic Warfare Capabilities

Chapter 6. External Support Activities

Appendix A. Joint Electronic Warfare Reports

Appendix B. Electronic Warfare Tab Format

Appendix C. Glossary

Appendix D. References

CHAPTER 1

Overview

As the modern battlespace has become more sophisticated, military operations are executed in an increasingly complex electromagnetic environment. While military forces use the electromagnetic spectrum to detect and identify enemy forces and to perform communications, surveillance, and weapons systems operations, both military forces and civilians use the electromagnetic spectrum for communications, navigation, information gathering, processing, storing, and reporting. This overlapping usage of the electromagnetic spectrum complicates the military's use of its electronic equipment and the military's gathering and security of military information.

Successful military operations now greatly depend on control of the electromagnetic spectrum. The force that can deprive the enemy the use of the electromagnetic spectrum, exploit the enemy's use of the electromagnetic spectrum to obtain information for its own purposes, and control the electromagnetic spectrum will have an important advantage. During a conflict, all commanders attempt to dominate the electromagnetic spectrum by targeting, exploiting, disrupting, degrading, deceiving, damaging, or destroying their opponent's electronic systems that support their military operations. Electronic warfare (EW) includes "any military action involving the use of electromagnetic and directed energy to control the electromagnetic spectrum or to attack the enemy." (Joint Publication [JP] 1-02) Electronic warfare is an important part of a military commander's arsenal of weapons. It allows a commander to provide electronic warfare support (ES), electronic attack (EA), and electronic protection (EP).

ELECTRONIC WARFARE SUPPORT

Electronic warfare support (ES) is the "division of electronic warfare involving actions tasked by, or under direct control of, an operational commander to search for, intercept, identify, and locate or localize sources of intentional and unintentional radiated electromagnetic energy for the purpose of immediate threat recognition, targeting, planning and conduct of future operations." (JP 1-02) The ES intelligence collection effort—

- Is used in peace, crisis, and war, which contributes to the building of an EW/intelligence database for planning and operations.

- Provides an all weather, day/night, long-range information gathering capability.
- Exploits an enemy's electromagnetic emissions and may provide information on enemy capabilities and intentions.
- Is covert and passive.
- Is a nonintrusive method of intelligence collection.

Electronic warfare support systems provide immediate threat recognition and are a source of information for immediate decisions involving electronic attack, electronic protection, avoidance, targeting, and other tactical employments of forces. Electronic warfare support systems collect data and produce information or intelligence that can be used to—

- Corroborate other sources of information or intelligence.
- Direct EA operations.
- Initiate self-protection measures.
- Task weapon systems for physical destruction.
- Support EP efforts.
- Create or modify EW databases.
- Support information operations (IO) activities.

Electronic warfare support data can be used to produce signals intelligence (SIGINT), provide targeting for electronic or destructive attack, and produce measurement and signature intelligence. Electronic warfare support and SIGINT both involve searching for, intercepting, identifying, and locating sources of intentional or unintentional radiated electromagnetic energy. The primary differences between the two are the detected information's intended use, the degree of analytical effort expended, the detail of information provided, and the timelines required. Electronic warfare support is conducted for immediate threat recognition and provides information required for immediate tactical decisions. Signals intelligence is used to gain information concerning the enemy, usually in response to an intelligence requirement. See MCWP 2-15.2, *Signals Intelligence*, for more information.

ELECTRONIC ATTACK

Electronic attack (EA) is "that division of electronic warfare involving the use of electromagnetic energy, directed energy, or antiradiation weapons to attack personnel, facilities, or equipment with the intent of degrading, neutralizing, or destroying enemy combat capability and is considered a form of fires." (JP 1-02)

Some common types of EA are spot, barrage, and sweep electromagnetic jamming. Electronic attack also includes various electromagnetic deception techniques such as false target or duplicate target generation.

Directed energy is "an umbrella term covering technologies that relate to the production of a beam of concentrated electromagnetic energy or atomic or subatomic particles." (JP 1-02) A directed-energy weapon is a system that uses "directed energy primarily as a direct means to damage or destroy an enemy's equipment, facilities, and personnel." (JP 1-02)

Antiradiation weapons are weapons that use radiated energy emitted from the target as their mechanism for guiding onto a targeted emitter (e.g., high speed antiradiation missile system [HARM]).

ELECTRONIC PROTECTION

Electronic protection (EP) is "that division of electronic warfare involving passive and active means taken to protect personnel, facilities, and equipment from any effects of friendly or enemy employment of electronic warfare that degrade, neutralize, or destroy friendly combat capability." (JP 1-02) In combat, electronic protection includes, but is not limited to, the application of good training and sound procedures for countering enemy electronic attack. United States forces (operators, users, and planners) must understand the enemy threat and the vulnerability of our electronic equipment to enemy EA efforts and ensure that appropriate actions are taken to safeguard our equipment from attack. To protect US forces, electronic protection must minimize an enemy's opportunity for successful ES and EA operations against US forces; therefore, it is necessary to—

- Regularly brief the EW threat to force personnel.
- Provide training on appropriate EP responses.
- Ensure that electronic system capabilities are safeguarded during exercises, workups, and pre-crisis training.

The technical aspects of EP must be considered when equipment acquisition programs are initiated. Equipment should be designed to limit inherent vulnerabilities. Additionally, these programs must be reviewed when EA vulnerabilities are detected.

Electronic protection measures include the selection of a scheme of maneuver that will minimize friendly electronic emissions that the enemy can intercept or disrupt using his ES and EA capabilities. Electronic protection can be accomplished through numerous methods; for example, a simple scheme of maneuver that can be executed with few or no emissions, by imposing radio silence or emission control (EMCON) procedures, by selecting avenues of approach that interposes terrain between friendly transmitters and enemy intercept stations. Electronic protection also includes measures to minimize the vulnerability of friendly receivers to enemy jamming; for example, reduced power, brevity of transmissions, and directional antennas.

SPECTRUM MANAGEMENT

Spectrum management plays a key role in the successful planning and execution of electronic warfare. Spectrum management includes "planning, coordinating, and managing joint use of the electromagnetic spectrum through operational, engineering, and administrative procedures. The objective of spectrum management is to enable electronic systems to perform their functions in the intended environment without causing or suffering unacceptable interference." (JP 1-02) Electronic warfare staff personnel have a major role to perform in the dynamic management of the electromagnetic spectrum during operations. Electronic warfare management activities are coordinated and deconflicted through the electronic warfare coordination cell (EWCC). The EWCC's primary mechanism for spectrum management is the restricted frequency list (RFL), which identifies friendly and enemy frequencies that cannot be jammed for various reasons. For further guidance on electromagnetic spectrum use, see Chairman of the Joint Chiefs of Staff Instruction (CJCSI) 3320.01, *Electromagnetic Spectrum Use in Joint Military Operations*. For specific guidance on reporting and controlling electromagnetic interference, see CJCSI 3320.02A, *Joint Spectrum Interference Resolution (JSIR)*.

CHAPTER 2

Command and Control

The commander is the focal point for the conduct of operations, and his staff is the central coordinating authority. Electronic warfare falls under the staff cognizance of the staff operations officer (G-3/S-3). The commander and his staff are supported by the EWCC. The EWCC—if it is established—plans, synchronizes, coordinates, and deconflicts all EW operations for the MAGTF. The EWCC's composition is dictated by the size of the force, the mission, and the available EW resources. Although electronic warfare is coordinated through the EWCC, individual EW units have responsibilities that include—

- Developing an EW concept of operations.
- Planning and coordinating EW-related activities.
- Developing supporting plans.
- Supporting the operational maneuver of the MAGTF.
- Synchronizing ES, EA, and EP activities.

The staffs of individual EW units are assigned EW functions in order to assist the commander in his planning and conduct of EW operations. Commanders and their staffs must ensure that thorough and continuous coordination is maintained to ensure that electronic warfare employed against an enemy threat will not unacceptably degrade friendly use of the electromagnetic spectrum.

CONTROL TASKS

Control of EW operations is essential; it allows optimal friendly use of the electromagnetic spectrum while targeting the enemy in a manner that supports the operational scheme of maneuver. However, control may become difficult to manage during joint operations or operations involving the participation of allied forces. Electronic warfare is broadly controlled by establishing measures to ensure the coordination of EW activities between forces; establishing procedures to monitor the execution of EW activities; and finally, by establishing a means to assess the effectiveness of EW operations, to maintain the EW estimate, and to recommend and implement changes. Electronic warfare control tasks include the following:

Coordinating EW operations

- Coordinate actions and operations within the parameters of the designated authority.
- Direct action within established timelines and conditions.
- Coordinate actions and operations, where lines of authority and responsibility overlap or conflict in order to advise units of adjacent or related actions and operations, direct supporting operations, and resolve conflicts.
- Coordinate/deconflict EA operations with the joint restricted frequency list (JRFL).
- Coordinate with planned IO, to include deception, destruction, psychological operations, and operations security (OPSEC).
- Coordinate continuing administrative, logistic, communications, and external agency support for EW operations.

Monitoring EW operations

- Monitor ES operations:
  - Execute operational tasking authority, in accordance with SIGINT.
  - Provide information or feedback for analysis of the effectiveness of IO.
  - Monitor dissemination of electronic warfare support to support electronic attack and electronic protection.
- Monitor EA operations:
  - Maintain positive control of EA operations.
  - Ensure integration with the targeting process.
- Monitor EP operations:
  - OPSEC assessment and OPSEC plan.
  - Communications security (COMSEC) monitoring operations.
  - EW reprogramming, as required.

Assessing effectiveness of EW operations

- Electronic warfare support:
  - Search for, intercept, identify, and locate sources of radiated electromagnetic energy.

- ○ Provide near real time threat recognition in support of immediate operational decisions involving electronic attack, electronic protection, avoidance, targeting, or other tactical employment of forces.
- Electronic attack:
  - ○ Focus on offensive use of the electromagnetic spectrum to directly attack enemy combat capability.
  - ○ Coordinate EW with military deception plans (timing, message, feed-back mechanism).
  - ○ Use directed energy and antiradiation missiles.
- Electronic protection:
  - ○ Protect personnel, facilities, and equipment from effects of friendly or enemy electronic warfare.
  - ○ Employ COMSEC measures.
  - ○ Employ EMCON measures.
  - ○ Employ wartime reserve modes.
  - ○ Reassess operational and tactical measures and countermeasures.
  - ○ Coordinate EW reprogramming.

Maintaining EW estimate

- Review/revise EW course of action (COA) in support of current and future operations:
  - ○ Coordinate with G-2/S-2 and G-6/S-6.
  - ○ Integrate electronic warfare into the targeting cycle.
  - ○ Integrate electronic warfare into the battle damage assessment.
  - ○ Integrate electronic warfare into the fires plan.
- Review/revise ES COA:
  - ○ Integrate electronic warfare support with intelligence cycle.
  - ○ Integrate electronic warfare support with collection plan.
- Review/revise EA COA:
  - ○ Integrate electromagnetic deception in support of military deception, as required.
  - ○ Review operational effect of tactical jamming and destructive electronic attack.

○ Submit targets for re-attack and for suppression as required.

- Review/revise EP COA:

  ○ Integrate electronic warfare with OPSEC and SIGINT efforts.

  ○ Coordinate electronic warfare with RFL/JRFL.

- War game EW COAs.

Recommending changes to EW operations

- Ensure EW operations maintain currency with MAGTF commander's intent.

- Coordinate EW operations with tactical operations.

- Integrate electronic warfare within the scope of IO.

ELECTRONIC WARFARE COORDINATION CELL

The EWCC facilitates coordination of EW operations with other fires, communications and information systems use, and intelligence operations. Additionally, EW participation in IO is accomplished through the EWCC. The EWCC identifies conflicts in planned operations and coordinates efforts by the G-2/S-2, G-3/S-3, and G-6/S-6.

The EWCC is under the staff cognizance of the G-3/S-3, and MAGTF staffs provide personnel to form the EWCC. The EWCC may include an electronic warfare officer (EWO), a communications and information systems representative, and other liaison officers as needed. Liaison could include radio battalion (RadBn) representation, airborne electronic countermeasures officers, a representative from the Marine air control group, and other Service representatives. Personnel are also provided for liaison teams to higher headquarter's EW coordination organizations when required, such as the joint force commander's electronic warfare staff (JCEWS) or IO cell that may be created within a joint task force (JTF).

The EWCC's structure is determined by, but not limited to, the overall structure of the combatant force and the level of electronic warfare to be conducted. The EWCC unifies Marine Corps EW functions. It does not add structure to an existing organization but it is used to coordinate EW activities of personnel already assigned. For example:

- In a highly complex joint suppression of enemy air defenses (J-SEAD) operation, EWCC personnel may be required to coordinate with representatives from the other Services and operational forces (air defense, maneuver units, and artillery) to plan and execute an operation.

- A less complicated operation may include limited jamming that is managed by the EW staff with minimum outside coordination required.

Electronic warfare coordination cell functions and responsibilities are as follows:

- Coordinates, synchronizes, and deconflicts EW targeting with fire support, intelligence collection plans, and operations.
- Ensures that electronic warfare is considered in each phase of the operation plan (OPLAN)/operation order (OPORD).
- Integrates electronic warfare into the IO portions of OPLANs/OPORDs.
- Ensures that the command's EW operations support the JTF campaign plan.
- Recommends the level of EW tasking of subordinate commands to the G-3/S-3.
- Assists the G-6/S-6 in the compilation of the RFL and the JRFL and resolves any conflicts.
- Resolves potential EW fratricide and misidentification issues.
- Coordinates subordinate command's request for electronic warfare support.
- Coordinates requests for electronic warfare support from other Services and allies.
- Establishes procedures for the rapid exchange of EW information to support planning and execution.
- Assesses the effects of friendly and enemy EW activity on the battlefield.
- Maintains the status of EW resources available to the commander.
- Identifies EW requirements for intelligence support.
- Coordinates EW reprogramming activities.
- Coordinates the administrative and logistic support and communications requirements of tailored EW packages that support time-phased force and deployment data.

OPERATIONS STAFF (G-3/S-3)

The operations staff has the responsibility for planning, coordinating, and supervising EW activities, except for intelligence. The operations staff is responsible for—

- Exercising electronic warfare, on behalf of the commander, through the issuance of OPORDs.
- Tasking assigned and attached EW units through the EWCC.

- Exercising control over electronic attack, including integration of electromagnetic deception plans.
- Coordinating EW training with other requirements.

INTELLIGENCE STAFF (G-2/S-2)

The intelligence staff advises the commander and his staff on the intelligence aspects of electronic warfare. The intelligence staff is responsible for—

- Tasking EW units in accordance with the intelligence collection plan.
- Providing intelligence on enemy organizations, locations, and capabilities.
- Assisting in the preparation of the intelligence-related portion of the EW estimate.
- Disseminating EW intelligence.
- Providing advice on the RFL by recommending guarded frequencies.
- Maintaining appropriate EW databases.

COMMUNICATIONS-ELECTRONICS STAFF (G-6/S-6)

The communications-electronics staff is the coordinator of the electromagnetic spectrum for a wide variety of communications and electronics resources. It is responsible for—

- Issuing communications-electronics operating instructions.
- Preparing EP policy on behalf of the commander.
- Coordinating the preparation of the RFL and issuance of EMCON guidance.
- Assisting in the preparation of EW plans and tabs.
- Coordinating frequency allocation, assignment, and use.
- Coordinating electromagnetic deception plans and operations in which assigned communications resources participate.
- Coordinating measures to reduce electromagnetic interference.
- Reporting all enemy EA activity to the EWCC for counteraction.

INFORMATION OPERATIONS CELL

On many joint staffs, the intra-staff coordination previously accomplished through a JCEWS has been replaced by an IO cell or similar organization. The IO cell, if established, coordinates EW activities with other IO activities in order to maximize effect and prevent mutual interference. An EWCC representative may be assigned to the IO cell to facilitate coordination. For more information about the organization and procedures of the IO cell, see JP 3-13, *Joint Doctrine for Information Operations.*

OPERATIONS CONTROL AND ANALYSIS CENTER

The operations control and analysis center (OCAC) provides centralized direction, management, and control of SIGINT and ground EW activities within the Marine expeditionary force (MEF) and coordinates with the MEF EWCC and external national assets. Operations control and analysis center personnel process, analyze, and disseminate collected information. The OCAC is located within the MEF headquarters near other intelligence agencies. It provides an interface between the RadBn and the MEF G-2/S-2. The OCAC coordinates ground EW activities with the EWCC. While typically established to support a MEF, an OCAC may be established for any size MAGTF.

CHAPTER 3

Planning

The MAGTF campaign is the synchronization of air, land, and sea operations in harmony with diplomatic, economic, and informational efforts in order to attain national objectives. The EW component of any operation requires early integration within the MAGTF and also with external agencies. Electronic warfare planning is conducted simultaneously with operational planning through the Marine Corps Planning Process (MCPP).

The MCPP is an internal planning process that supports decisionmaking by the MAGTF commander. It aligns with and complements the joint deliberate and crisis action planning processes. The MCPP is applicable to all echelons of command and across the range of military operations. The MCPP establishes procedures for analyzing a mission, developing and wargaming COAs against the threat, comparing friendly COAs against the commander's criteria and other friendly COAs, selecting a COA, preparing an OPORD/OPLAN for execution, and transitioning the OPORD/OPLAN to those tasked with its execution. The MCPP organizes these procedures into six manageable, logical steps: mission analysis, COA development, COA war game, COA comparison and decision, orders development, and transition.

Electronic warfare planning occurs concurrently with other operational planning during the MCPP and supports the operational maneuver of the MAGTF (see the following table). Electronic warfare planning is normally accomplished by the EWCC and is led by the G-3/S-3's staff EWO with representatives from the G-2/S-2 and G-6/S-6.

Electronic Warfare and the Marine Corps Planning Process.

MCPP Steps	EW Planning Action
Mission Analysis	Review commander's guidance.
	Review rules of engagement (ROE).
	Identify commander's critical information requirements, priority intelligence requirements, essential elements of friendly information.
	Coordinate internal liaison.
	Request external augmentation as required.
	Identify the enemy's operational centers of gravity.
	Develop the EW estimate.
	Produce the EW mission statement.
	Determine EA, ES, and EP objectives.
COA Development	Conduct intelligence gain/loss review.
	Consider special IO.
	Model EW effects.
	Integrate with operational maneuver.
	Determine command relationships.
COA War Game	Utilize automated models.
	War game in conjunction with other IO COAs.
COA Comparison and Decision	Brief MAGTF commander and G-3/S-3.
Orders Development	Develop Tab B (Electronic Warfare) to Appendix 3 (Information Operations/Command and Control Warfare) to Annex C (Operations).
Transition	Publish OPORD.
	Integrate electronic warfare support into MAGTF intelligence cycle.
	Integrate electronic warfare support and electronic attack into MAGTF targeting cycle.
	Integrate electronic warfare support and electronic attack into MAGTF battle damage assessment cycle.
	Monitor/control EW operations.

PLANNING FACTORS

Electronic warfare planning factors include the following:

- Consider requirements for friendly communications, navigation systems, targeting systems, and radar with respect to the anticipated operations, expected tactical threat, and electromagnetic interference considerations. Once identified, these requirements should be entered into the RFL under appropriate categories (e.g., TABOO, RESTRICTED).

- Identifiy information security, COMSEC, and electronic security measures necessary to deny OPSEC indicators to enemy electromagnetic sensors.

- Developing the RFL (or during joint operations the JRFL) is critical to ensuring deconfliction of EA and ES activities.

- Coordinate and identify specific resources required for interference deconfliction.

- Identify commander's critical information requirements that support commanders and EW operations and facilitate electronic warfare support, which must be included in Annex B (Intelligence) to the OPORD.

- Coordinate and establish procedures to ensure timely fulfillment of information requirements, including tactical, real-time dissemination.

- Review ROE to determine what restrictions may be placed on EW operations.

REQUEST AND APPROVAL OF EW SUPPORT

Requests for EW support are forwarded through the chain of command to the commander authorized to plan and conduct EW operations. For ground EA operations that involve RadBn assets, the MAGTF commander is usually the authorizing commander. For airborne EA operations supported by EA-6Bs, the aviation combat element (ACE) commander is usually the authorizing commander. The commander authorized to conduct electronic warfare makes a tentative decision on whether or not to provide the requested support. This tentative decision is based on such things as the relative importance of the tactical activity being supported, competing requests, and the adequacy of the technical database to support the request. Once the request is coordinated with the EWCC, the tentative decision is finalized and passed to the supporting EW unit.

For support requests involving electronic attack, the commander requesting EA support describes only the friendly operation to be supported. The commander requesting EA support does not list the enemy's frequencies and stations to be attacked because communications systems are usually complex and consist of several channels for passing requests for fires, requests for reinforcements, intelligence reports, and other critical messages. Therefore, the EWCC, in coordination with the MAGTF G-2/S-2, better understands the enemy's communications systems and can design EA plans that support friendly operations.

Support requests involving electronic warfare support are initiated by establishing commander's critical information requirements and priority intelligence requirements. The MAGTF G-2/S-2 uses the process of collection management to convert these information requirements into collection requirements, establish priorities, task or coordinate with appropriate collection sources or agencies, monitor results, and retask ES assets as appropriate. Collection management ensures that MAGTF ES requirements are met through the most efficient use of collection assets.

See appendix A for joint EW report formats.

STAFFING, COORDINATION, AND APPROVAL OF THE ELECTRONIC WARFARE PLAN

Electronic warfare plans developed by EW units attached to the MAGTF headquarters or to one of its elements are submitted to the EWCC. The EWO staffs these plans within the headquarters and to adjacent, supporting, and higher headquarters. The communications-electronics officer reviews the plans to ensure that they will not disrupt command and control communications. The G-2/S-2 reviews the plans to ensure that they will not needlessly disrupt or stop collection of critical information and intelligence. Problems that arise during staffing that cannot be resolved are referred to the commander or his designated representative, usually the G-3/S-3. Once all problems are identified and reconciled, the decision is made whether or not to execute the EW plan and, if so, when.

Electronic warfare plans developed by adjacent, supported, and supporting headquarters should be coordinated by these headquarters with the MAGTF headquarters. The EWO staffs these plans within the MAGTF in coordination with the G-2/S-2, G-3/S-3, and G-6/S-6. In the event of operational conflict, the headquarters that originated the plan is advised of the problem and attempts resolve any conflicts. Problems that cannot be resolved are referred to a higher authority for reconciliation.

ELECTRONIC WARFARE ELEMENTS OF THE OPERATION ORDER

Once the EW plan is approved, it is documented in the OPORD. The OPORD contains EW planning guidance, a description of planned EW operations, and information on spectrum management. For more information on OPORDs, see MCWP 5-1, *Marine Corps Planning Process,* and Chairman of the Joint Chiefs of Staff Manual (CJCSM) 3122.03, *Joint Operation Planning and Execution System, Volume II, Planning Formats and Guidance.*

Electronic Warfare Planning Guidance

Electronic warfare planning guidance may be included in the OPORD as a tab to Appendix 3 (Information Operations/Command and Control Warfare) of Annex C (Operations) of the OPORD.

Electronic Warfare Operations

Electronic warfare operations are included as Tab B (Electronic Warfare) to Appendix 3 (Information Operations/Command and Control Warfare) to Annex C (Operations) of the OPORD. The EW tab should—

- Summarize the scope of EW operations and methods to be employed, including the employment of organic and nonorganic capabilities.
- Identify the desired electromagnetic profile selected by the commander for the basic concept of operations and provide EMCON guidance to commanders so that the desired electromagnetic and acoustic profiles are realized.
- Identify EW resources required to support IO, suppression of enemy air defenses (SEAD), and other elements and activities of IO.
- Evaluate enemy threats to critical friendly command and control, communications, weapons control systems, target acquisition systems, intelligence and surveillance systems, and computer networks.
- Specify EP measures necessary to ensure effective operations during combat.

See appendix B for an example of the EW tab.

Spectrum Management

Since electronic warfare occurs in the electromagnetic spectrum, EW planners must closely coordinate their efforts with those members of the staff who manage military use of the electromagnetic spectrum. EW planners use the RFL as a key tool to perform spectrum management. The RFL is normally found in Annex K (Communications and Information Systems) of the OPORD. For additional guidance on spectrum management, see CJSCM 3320.01, *Joint Operations in the Electromagnetic Battlespace.*

BATTLESPACE CONSIDERATIONS

Expeditionary Electronic Warfare

The commander, landing force designates a landing force EWO who will be responsible for the coordination and control of EW operations ashore and for the preparation of the EW input to the landing force OPORD/OPLAN. An EWCC may be established to provide the EWO an EW coordinating mechanism.

When an amphibious force is formed and the commander, landing force is afloat, a landing force EWCC may be established afloat to coordinate EW plans and operations with the Navy's EWO. During amphibious and littoral operations, the AF EWO continues to function in support of the amphibious task force and the EWCC functions in support of the landing force. However, close coordination of EW operations remains necessary. The initiating directive may require that coordination of EW operations be retained afloat or be transferred to an EWCC of an appropriate headquarters ashore. For more information on command and control during amphibious operations, see JP 3-02, *Joint Doctrine for Amphibious Operations.*

Ground Electronic Warfare

Ground electronic warfare supports the operational scheme of maneuver and is employed as the MAGTF commander deems necessary. Generally, ground EW equipment is employed on a highly mobile platform (e.g., mobile electronic warfare support system [MEWSS] product improvement program [PIP]) and should be as survivable and mobile as the force it supports. Ground electronic warfare is primarily directed against tactical communications systems. Due to the short-range nature of tactical signals direction finding, EA sites are usually located in the forward area of the battlefield, either with or near forward units.

To be effective, ground electronic warfare requires the following:

- Protection from enemy ground and aviation elements by the supported unit.
- Logistical support.
- Clear identification of EW requirements of the supported commander.

Ground EW capabilities are as follows:

- Supports ground units operations directly.
- Provides continuous operations.
- Responds to EW requirements of supported ground commander.

- Provides electromagnetic jamming of enemy air defenses and enemy command, control, and communications systems in support of aviation or ground units.

Ground electronic warfare has the following limitations:

- Vulnerable to enemy attack.
- Can be masked by terrain.
- Distance/propagation characteristics of enemy electronic systems.
- Vulnerable to electronic protection actions employed by the enemy.
- Vulnerable to enemy electromagnetic deception measures.

Airborne Electronic Warfare

While ground and airborne EW planning and execution are similar, the most significant difference is the shortened airborne EW employment time. Aviation operations are generally much shorter in duration and conducted at much higher speeds than ground operations. Therefore, the timeliness of EW support is critical to aviation operations. Aviation EW support may require a more extensive database and a more detailed plan than is required for ground operations. Additionally, airborne ES activities are usually conducted in general support of the MAGTF or the JTF.

To be effective, airborne electronic warfare requires the following:

- Clear understanding of the supported commander's EW needs.
- Airborne EA and ES operations require detailed planning and integration in order to be successful against modern air defenses.
- Ground support facilities.
- Liaison between the aircrews of the aircraft providing the EW support and the aircrews being supported.
- Protection from enemy aircraft.

Airborne EW capabilities are as follows:

- Provides direct support to other tactical aviation missions.
- Provides extended EW range over that offered by ground assets.
- Possesses greater mobility and flexibility than ground assets.
- Supports ground units or the MAGTF in general support and in coordination with the RadBn.

Airborne electronic warfare has the following limitations:

- Limited assets (nonorganic platforms, specifically designed to perform electronic warfare, may need to be requested to support the MAGTF through JTF/theater commander).
- Time on station considerations.
- Vulnerable to enemy EP actions.
- Vulnerable to enemy electromagnetic deception.
- Line-of-sight limitations (although the effective ranges at which electronic warfare support and electronic attack can be conducted by aircraft are far greater than those of ground EW assets).

FUNCTIONAL CONSIDERATIONS

Electronic Warfare Support Considerations

There is a mutually supporting relationship between intelligence and electronic warfare support. Intelligence feeds electronic warfare support by making accurate electronic order of battle information available in order to accurately program ES equipment, such as radar warning and tactical jamming systems. Alternatively, electronic warfare support feeds intelligence through ES systems that collect information. The information can then be rapidly disseminated as a threat warning or may be passed to intelligence production and analysis elements for further processing.

Electronic warfare support provides immediate threat recognition and a source of information for immediate decisions involving electronic attack, electronic protection, avoidance, targeting, and other tactical employment of forces. Specific examples of ES capabilities include radar warning equipment installed on tactical aircraft for self-defense, the receiver suite of the tactical jamming system on board EW aircraft (e.g., EA-6B), and the receiver suite in ground EA support systems (e.g., MEWSS PIP). To best meet immediate tactical requirements, ES information used in immediate threat recognition is rapidly disseminated without in-depth processing.

Concurrent with threat warning reporting, information derived from electronic warfare support is also provided to MAGTF intelligence production and analysis elements. After analysis and integration with other sources of information, ES information becomes intelligence and is released as a form of intelligence reporting through normal intelligence channels to the MAGTF and to external units or agencies.

To ensure that the intelligence needs of tactical commanders are met, processed ES information or intelligence products may be passed directly to a tactical unit. This information may also be passed by a signals intelligence support unit (SSU) from the RadBn or may take the form of reports that are generated by the tactical electronic reconnaissance processing and evaluation system (TERPES) and passed by the Marine tactical electronic warfare squadron (VMAQ). In either case, clear procedures and guidelines must be established to coordinate intelligence dissemination within the MAGTF. For more information on intelligence dissemination and reporting, see MCWP 2-1, *Intelligence Operations*, and MCWP 2-15.2.

Electronic Attack Considerations

Electronic attack operations may be preplanned or conducted in response to the immediate tactical situation. If commanders and their staffs use electromagnetic jamming, they must carefully weigh the operational requirement against the ROE, the affects on friendly systems, and the loss of enemy information otherwise obtained by ES measures. Degradation of some friendly communications may have to be accepted in order to effectively employ jamming.

Some key planning considerations for EA operations include authorization, jamming control, and timing. Since the results of electronic warfare can be profound and far-reaching, EW planners and operators must understand both peacetime and wartime ROE and EW operations cannot be executed without proper authorization. Because of its possible impact on friendly communications and noncommunications emitters (e.g., radars, data links), jamming will normally require a centralized controlling authority. However, in certain situations, jamming control, with its incumbent authority, may be delegated to lower commanders. Jamming may only be effective for a limited time because the enemy may take the necessary measures to overcome the effects of jamming or attempt to use electronic protection to overcome the MAGTF's jamming effects.

Jamming achieves its best results when resources are concentrated to simultaneously disrupt or degrade all types of electromagnetic communications and/or noncommunications systems of selected enemy units, formations, or weapons systems that have a direct impact on the accomplishment of the mission. Jamming's maximum effectiveness is obtained if the attack is delivered at a critical time against a critical enemy electronic system (e g , fire control nets during his attack, air defense systems during friendly offensive air operations, command and control communications for the control of the movement or commitment of reserves). The indiscriminate employment of jamming must be avoided because it may alert the enemy to impending operations in specific areas.

Jamming's greatest weakness is that it may indicate knowledge of the enemy's frequencies, which allows him, if capable, to change his frequencies and make further jamming difficult and electronic warfare support less productive. Therefore, jamming for the purpose of harassing the enemy or supporting a minor operation is counterproductive because it assists the enemy in determining his vulnerability to jamming and it helps him recognize and adjust to our jamming capabilities.

Electronic Protection Considerations

Electronic protection protects personnel, facilities, and equipment from any friendly or enemy employment of electronic warfare that could degrade, neutralize, or destroy friendly combat capability. Electronic protection includes physical security, information security, COMSEC measures, transmission security, and EMCON measures. It also includes the detection and response to hostile actions against friendly force's information systems. The following key functions must be considered when planning for EP operations:

- Information security, including its two disciplines of computer security and communications security.
- Vulnerability analysis and assessment, which forms the basis for formulating EP plans. (The Defense Information Systems Agency operates a program known as the Vulnerability Analysis and Assessment Program specifically focusing on automated information systems.)
- Monitoring and feedback. (The National Security Agency [NSA] has a COMSEC monitoring program that focuses on telecommunications systems using wire and electronic communications.)

For additional information on EP-related measures, see CJCSI 6510.01B, *Information Assurance and Computer Network Defense.*

Electronic Warfare Reprogramming Considerations

Electronic warfare reprogramming is the deliberate alteration or modification of friendly EW or target sensing systems in response to validated changes in enemy equipment and tactics or to the electromagnetic environment. The reprogramming of EW and target sensing system equipment is the responsibility of each Service or organization through its respective EW reprogramming support programs. It includes changes to self-defense systems, offensive weapons systems, and intelligence collection systems. During joint operations, swift identification and reprogramming efforts are critical in a rapidly evolving hostile situation. The key consideration for EW reprogramming is joint coordination. Joint coordination of Service reprogramming efforts is required to ensure that reprogramming requirements are identified, processed, and implemented in a consistent manner by all friendly forces. For more information on EW reprogramming, see JP 3-51, *Joint Doctrine for Electronic Warfare*.

Electromagnetic Deception Considerations

Electromagnetic deception "is the deliberate radiation, reradiation, alteration, suppression, absorption, denial, enhancement, or reflection of electromagnetic energy in a manner intended to convey misleading information to an enemy or to enemy electromagnetic-dependent weapons, thereby degrading or neutralizing the enemy's combat capability." (JP 3-51) Manipulative electromagnetic deception, simulative electromagnetic deception, and imitative electromagnetic deception are all types of electromagnetic deception.

Electromagnetic deception operations, like electromagnetic jamming, normally require centralized coordination and control and should be conducted as part of an overall deception plan. Missions are normally preplanned but may be immediate if opportunities for limited application become available. However, all electromagnetic deception operations require specific authorization from the senior headquarters controlling the operation.

Large-scale electromagnetic deception operations may be expensive in terms of preparation time and resources. Deception efforts are more likely to succeed if designed to achieve a specific objective that is limited in time and scope; therefore, the MAGTF may use limited-scale deception operations at selected key times in the operation.

For more information on the types of electromagnetic deception, see JP 3-51.

Joint-Suppression of Enemy Air Defenses Considerations

Suppression of enemy air defenses is a specific type of mission that "neutralizes, destroys, or temporarily degrades surface-based enemy air defenses by destructive and/or disruptive means." (JP 1-02) The term J-SEAD includes all SEAD activities provided by one component of the joint force in support of another. Suppression of enemy air defenses missions are of critical importance to the success of any operation where control of the air is contested by the enemy and relies on a variety of EW platforms to conduct electronic warfare support, electronic protection, and electronic attack.

The key planning consideration for J-SEAD is joint coordination. Electronic warfare planners should coordinate closely with joint and component air planners to ensure that electronic warfare is integrated into J-SEAD missions and given priority in the overall EW plan. Given the fundamental importance of control of the air in any joint operation, care should be taken that EW assets required for J-SEAD missions are appropriately allocated between J-SEAD and other EW missions (e.g., communications jamming), particularly during that portion of an operation when control of the air is being established. For more information about J-SEAD, see JP 3-01.4, *Joint Tactics, Techniques, and Procedures for Joint Suppression of Enemy Air Defenses (J-SEAD)*.

CHAPTER 4

Joint and Multinational Operations

In joint operations, the various armed forces of the US military work together to accomplish a mission. In multinational operations, forces of two or more nations work together to accomplish the mission. In either type of operation, all forces operate in accordance with guidelines that establish organizational frameworks and facilitate coordination. Joint operations are guided by US joint doctrine established by the Department of Defense (DOD) (e.g., JP 3-51). Multinational forces (MNFs) conduct operations based on established international standards, such as policy and doctrine established through the North Atlantic Treaty Organization (NATO) (e.g., Allied Joint Pub [AJP] 3-6, *Allied Joint Electronic Warfare Doctrine*). While some multinational organizations are permanently organized with established relationships and procedures, like NATO, other temporary coalitions last only for the duration of a crisis and must cooperatively develop a concept of EW support to meet their common mission.

JOINT OPERATIONS

Joint operations generally increase the complexity of EW operations. EW coordination becomes increasingly difficult as additional units and agencies become involved in the planning and execution of electronic warfare. Joint task forces are task-organized and their composition varies. Although their structure is situationally dependent, the EW organization within the joint force normally centers on the joint force staff, the component commands, the JCEWS and/or an IO cell, and supporting joint centers (e.g., the joint operations center [JOC], joint intelligence center [JIC], joint frequency management office [JFMO], and joint targeting coordination board [JTCB]).

Joint Force Staff of the Joint Task Force

The joint force staff operations director (J-3) has primary staff responsibility for EW activity and for planning, coordinating, and integrating joint EW operations with other combat disciplines within the JTF. A JCEWS and/or an IO cell are normally formed to assist the J-3. The joint force staff intelligence director (J-2) is responsible for timely collection, processing, tailoring, and dissemination of all-source intelligence for electronic warfare. The joint force staff communications-electronics director (J-6) has primary staff responsibility for coordinating the use of the entire electromagnetic spectrum for command, control, communications, and computers (C4) systems and electromagnetic-dependent weapons systems employed by the joint force.

Joint Task Force Component Commands

During joint operations, operational control of EW assets is exercised through JTF component commanders. Each component is organized and equipped to conduct EW tasks in support of its basic missions and the joint force commander's (JFC's) campaign objectives.

The JFC normally designates a joint force air component commander (JFACC) to provide unity of effort for employing air power in support of his objectives. The JFC specifies the JFACC's responsibilities and level of authority. Normally, the JFACC plans, coordinates, allocates, and tasks air forces (including EW capable air assets) based on the JFC's apportionment decisions. However, the MAGTF commander always retains operational control of organic MAGTF air assets.

Joint Commanderís Electronic Warfare Staff

A JCEWS supports the JFC in the planning, coordination, and integration of joint force EW operations. The JCEWS's focus is to deny the enemy the use of the electromagnetic spectrum while maintaining its availability for friendly use. The JCEWS ensures that joint EW capabilities support the JFC's objectives.

The JCEWS is an element within the J-3, and it is composed of representatives from each of the components of the joint force. It will be headed by an EWO, who is appointed by the J-3. The JCEWS includes representatives from the J-2 and J-6 to facilitate intelligence support and EW frequency deconfliction. Support teams from various organizations can be requested to assist the JCEWS.

On many joint staffs, the intra-staff coordination previously accomplished through a joint commander's EW staff is now performed by an IO cell or similar organization. The IO cell, if established, coordinates EW activities with other IO activities in order to maximize effectiveness and prevent mutual interference. If both a JCEWS and an IO cell exist, a JCEWS representative may be assigned to the IO cell to facilitate coordination. For more information about the organization and procedures of the IO cell, see JP 3-13.

Joint Operations Center

The JFC normally organizes a JOC to serve as the focal point for operational matters. The JOC battlestaff, directed by the J-3, is comprised of representatives from the directorates within the joint headquarters (e.g., J-1, J-2, J-3, J-6).

Joint Intelligence Center

The JIC is the focal point for the intelligence structure supporting the J-2. Directed by the J-2, the JIC communicates directly with component intelligence agencies and monitors intelligence support to EW operations. The JIC has the capability to adjust intelligence gathering to support the EW mission.

Joint Frequency Management Office

Each geographic combatant commander is tasked by joint policy to establish a frequency management structure that includes a JFMO and to establish procedures that support ongoing operations. The JFMO may be assigned from the supported combatant commander's J-6 staff, from a component's staff, or from an external command such as the Joint Spectrum Center (JSC). The JFMO is responsible for coordinating the C4 system use of the electromagnetic spectrum, frequency management, and frequency deconfliction. The JFMO develops the frequency management plan and makes recommendations to alleviate mutual interference.

Joint Targeting Coordination Board

The JTCB typically reviews target information, develops targeting guidance and priorities, and prepares and refines joint target lists if needed. The JTCB monitors the effectiveness of targeting efforts, coordinates and deconflicts all JTF targeting operations, validates no-fire areas, and approves new target nominations for inclusion in the joint target list.

MULTINATIONAL OPERATIONS

Electronic warfare is an integral part of multinational operations, and US planners must be prepared to integrate US and allied or coalition EW capabilities into a single, integrated EW plan. US planners should also be capable of providing allied or coalition nations with information concerning US EW capabilities and providing EW planning and operational support to allied or coalition nations. However, the planning of MNF electronic warfare is difficult due to security issues, differences in levels of training, language barriers, and terminology and procedural issues. US and NATO EW doctrine attempt to provide commonality and a framework for the employment of electronic warfare in NATO operations, see AJP 3.6 for specific information.

Multinational Force Commander

The MNF commander provides guidance for planning and conducting EW operations to the MNF through the J-3 and the EWCC, which is located at joint force headquarters. An IO cell may also be established to coordinate all IO-related activities, including related EW operations.

Multinational J-3 Staff

Within the multinational staff, the J-3 has primary responsibility for the planning and integration of EW activities. A staff EWO is designated, and his responsibilities include ensuring the integration of allied/coalition augmentees, ensuring that EW plans and procedures are properly interpreted/translated, coordinating appropriate communications connectivity, and integrating allied/coalition communications into a JRFL.

Electronic Warfare Coordination Cell

In multinational operations, the EWCC is the JFC's mechanism for coordinating EW resources within the joint operations area. It should be established as an integral part of the multinational joint force headquarters J-3 staff, at whatever level is deemed appropriate, to provide an effective means of coordinating all EW activities by the MNF. The EWCC is responsible for planning and coordinating all in-theater EW activities in close liaison with the J2, J5, and J6.

Electronic Warfare Mutual Support

Electronic warfare mutual support is a NATO term that is governed by Military Committee (MC) 64, *NATO EW Policy*. Electronic warfare mutual support is the timely exchange of EW information in order to make the best use of the available resources. It is facilitated by the use of an agreed reference database called the NATO emitter database. Electronic warfare mutual support procedures developed as a result of EW planning should include:

- A review of friendly and enemy information data elements that may be exchanged.
- Mechanisms leading to the exchange of data during peace, crisis, and war.
- Development of peacetime exercises to practice the exchange of data.
- Establishment of EW points of contact with adjacent formations and higher and subordinate headquarters for planning purposes, regardless of whether EW resources exist or not.
- Initial acquisition and maintenance of allied forces EW capabilities.
- Exchange of EW liaison teams equipped with appropriate communications.

- Establishment and rehearsal of contingency plans for the exchange of information on friendly and enemy forces.

- Development of communications protocols in accordance with NATO Standardization Agreement (STANAG) 5048, *The Minimum Scale of Connectivity for Communications and Information Systems for NATO Land Forces.*

- Provision of secure, dedicated, and survivable communications.

Other Considerations

Electronic Warfare Information Exchange. The development and use of joint information exchange protocols is essential to the planning and conduct of multinational EW operations.

Exchange of Signals Intelligence Information. Care should be taken not to violate SIGINT security rules when exchanging information. The policy and relationship between electronic warfare and SIGINT within NATO is set out in MC 64 and MC 101, *NATO SIGINT Policy.*

Exchange of Electronic Order of Battle. In peacetime, prior to formation of an MNF, the exchange of electronic order of battle information is normally achieved under bilateral agreement. During MNF operations, an EWCC representative, through the theater joint analysis center or JIC, ensures the maintenance of an up-to-date electronic order of battle. The inclusion of allied and coalition forces is based on security and information exchange guidelines. See MC 298, *Mutual SIGINT Support Between National and/or Multinational Tactical Formations Within NATO,* for more information on information exchange guidelines.

Electronic Warfare Reprogramming. EW reprogramming is a national responsibility. However, the MAGTF EWCC should be aware of reprogramming efforts being conducted within the MNF.

Information Operations. NATO policy for information operations is delineated in NATO publication MC 422, *NATO Policy for Information Operations.*

CHAPTER 5

MAGTF Electronic Warfare Capabilities

To provide EW support, the Marine Corps has two types of EW units: RadBns and VMAQs.

RADIO BATTALION

The mission of the RadBn is to provide COMSEC monitoring, tactical SIGINT, electronic warfare, and special intelligence communications support to the MAGTF. A RadBn's tasks include—

● Conducting interception; radio direction finding; recording and analysis of communications/noncommunications signals; and SIGINT processing, analysis, production, and reporting.

● Conducting electronic warfare against enemy or other hostile communications.

● Assisting in the protection of MAGTF communications from enemy exploitation by conducting COMSEC monitoring, analysis, and reporting on friendly force communications.

● Providing special intelligence communications support and cryptographic guard (personnel and terminal equipment) in support of the MAGTF command. (Normally, the communications unit supporting the MAGTF command element provides communications connectivity for special intelligence communications.)

● Providing task-organized detachments to MAGTFs with designated SIGINT, electronic warfare, special intelligence communications, and other required capabilities.

● Exercising technical control and direction over MAGTF SIGINT and EW operations.

● Providing radio reconnaissance teams with specialized insertion and extraction capabilities (e.g., combat rubber raiding craft, fast rope, rappel, helocast, static line parachute) to provide specified SIGINT and limited EA support during advance force, pre-assault, or deep post-assault operations.

● Coordinating technical SIGINT requirements and exchanging SIGINT technical information and material with national, theater, joint, and other SIGINT units.

- Providing intermediate, third, and fourth echelon maintenance of the RadBn's SIGINT and EW equipment.

Organization

The 1st RadBn, located at Marine Corps Base, Kaneohe Bay, HI, supports both I MEF and III MEF. The 2d RadBn, located at Camp Lejeune, NC, supports II MEF. Both battalions are organized and equipped along functional lines to provide administrative control of subordinate elements, to facilitate training, and to permit rapid structuring and operational deployment of task-organized units or detachments.

An entire RadBn will support a MEF operation. To support smaller MAGTFs, the RadBn is task-organized as an SSU. The SSU may be as large as a RadBn operational company or as small as a team of four Marines. A complete SSU contains all the capabilities found in a RadBn and consists of six basic elements: a command element; an operations, control, and analysis element; a collection and direction finding element; a special intelligence communications element; an EA element; and a service support element. The nature of the threat, specific mission tasking, and intelligence and operational requirements determine the composition and equipment of each element. For a complete description of RadBn organization, see MCWP 2-15.2.

The EA element conducts ground electronic attack for the MAGTF. It consists of the Marines and the equipment necessary to conduct ground EA operations. Personnel assigned to this element include EA supervisors or controllers and EA operators.

RadBn Electronic Attack Equipment

AN/ULQ-19(V)2 Electronic Attack Set. The AN/ULQ-19(V)2 electronic attack set allows operators to conduct spot or sweep jamming of single-channel voice or data signals operating in the standard military frequency range of 20 to 79.975 megahertz from selected mobile platforms (e.g. high mobility multipurpose wheeled vehicles, MEWSS, helicopters). When employed as a tactical, general purpose, low-VHF jamming system, the AN/ULQ-19(V)2 has a 250-watt radio frequency linear amplifier that produces a nominal 200 watts of effective radiated power using a standard omnidirectional whip antenna. To provide the required jamming, the system must be employed and operated from a location with an unobstructed signal line of sight to the target enemy's communications transceiver.

AN/MLQ-36 Mobile Electronic Warfare Support System. The AN/MLQ-36 MEWSS provides a multifunctional capability that gives SIGINT/EW operators limited armor protection. This equipment can provide SIGINT/EW support to highly mobile mechanized and military operations in urban terrain where maneuver and/or armor protection is critical. MEWSS consists of a signals intercept system, a radio direction finding system, an EA system, a secure communications system, and an intercom system installed in a logistic variant of the light armored vehicle.

AN/MLQ-36A Mobile Electronic Warfare Support System Product Improvement Program. The AN/MLQ-36A MEWSS PIP is an advanced SIGINT/EW system integrated into a light armored vehicle. The MEWSS PIP provides a total replacement of the EW mission equipment now fielded in the AN/MLQ-36 MEWSS. The MEWSS PIP provides the ability to detect and evaluate enemy communications emissions, detect and categorize enemy noncommunications emissions (e.g., battlefield radars), determine lines of bearing, and degrade enemy tactical radio communications during expeditionary operations. When mission-configured and working cooperatively with other MEWSS PIP platforms, the common suite of equipment can also provide precision location of battlefield emitters. The system is designed to have an automated tasking and reporting data link to other MAGTF assets such as the AN/TSQ-130 technical control and analysis center PIP. The MEWSS PIP and its future enhancements will provide the capability to exploit new and sophisticated enemy electronic emissions and conduct electronic attack in support of existing and planned national, theater, fleet, and MAGTF SIGINT/EW operations.

MARINE TACTICAL ELECTRONIC WARFARE SQUADRON

The Marine VMAQ's mission is to provide EW support to the MAGTF and other designated forces. The VMAQ conducts tactical jamming to prevent, delay, or disrupt the enemy's ability to use early warning, acquisition, fire or missile control, counterbattery, and battlefield surveillance radars. Tactical jamming also denies and/or degrades enemy communications capabilities. The VMAQ conducts electronic surveillance operations to maintain electronic orders of battle, including both selected emitter parameters and location of nonfriendly emitters. It also provides threat warnings for friendly aircraft, ships, and ground units. VMAQ tasks include—

- Providing airborne EA and ES support to the ACE and other designated operations by intercepting, recording, and jamming threat communications and noncommunications emitters.

- Processing, analyzing, and producing routine and time-sensitive electronic intelligence (ELINT) reports for updating and maintaining enemy electronic order of battle. This is accomplished through the EW division, which includes intelligence, TERPES, and the tactical EA-6B mission planning system (TEAMS). All are used to support pre-mission planning and post-mission processing of collected data and production of pertinent intelligence reports. Working in concert with squadron intelligence, TERPES and TEAMS provide required ELINT and electronic order of battle intelligence products to the ACE, MAGTF, and other requesting external agencies.
- Providing liaison personnel to higher staffs to assist in VMAQ employment planning.
- Providing an air EW liaison officer to the MAGTF EWCC.
- Conducting EA operations for EP training of MAGTF units.

Organization

There are four VMAQs (designated VMAQ-1 through VMAQ-4) assigned to Marine aircraft group-14, 2d Marine aircraft wing, Cherry Point, NC. Each squadron has five EA-6B Prowler aircraft. Each squadron is organized into administrative, intelligence/EW, operations, logistic, safety and standardization, and maintenance divisions.

VMAQ Electronic Attack Equipment

EA-6B Prowler. The EA-6B Prowler is a subsonic, all-weather, carrier-capable aircraft. The crew is composed of one pilot and three electronic countermeasure officers. The EA-6B's primary missions include collecting and processing designated threat signals of interest for jamming and subsequent processing, analysis, and intelligence reporting and employing the AGM-88 HARM against designated targets. The EA-6B's AN/ALQ-99 tactical jamming system effectively incorporates receivers for the reception of emitted signals and external jamming pods for the transmission of energy to jam victim radars (principally those associated with enemy air defense radars and associated command and control). In addition to the AN/ALQ-99, the EA-6B also employs the USQ-113 communications jammer to collect, record, and disrupt threat communications.

Tactical EA-6B Mission Planning System. TEAMS assists the EA-6B aircrew with planning and optimization of receivers, jammers, and HARM. TEAMS allows an operator to—

- Maintain area of operations emitter listings.
- Edit emitter parameters.

- Develop mission-specific geographic data and electronic order of battle to—

  ○ Tailor or create HARM direct attack libraries or manually modify entries/new threat cards for FA-18 HARM shooters.

  ○ Plan USQ-113 target selection.

- Perform post-flight mission analysis to—

  ○ Identify electronic emitters using various electronic parameter databases and ELINT analytical techniques.

  ○ Localize emitters by coordinates with a certain circular error of probability for each site.

  ○ Correlate new information with existing data.

  ○ Gather post-flight HARM information such as aircraft launch parameters, predicted seeker footprint, and whether the on board system detected a targeted signal at the time of impact.

Tactical Electronic Reconnaissance Processing and Evaluation System. The TERPES (AN/TSQ-90) is an air- and land-transportable, single-shelter ELINT processing and correlation system, and each of the four VMAQ squadrons includes a TERPES section. A TERPES section is composed of Marines, equipment, and software that identify and locate enemy radar emitters from data collected by EA-6B aircraft and those received from other intelligence sources, process and disseminate EW data rapidly to MAGTF and other intelligence centers, and provide mission planning and briefing support. TERPES support areas include operational support, intelligence analysis support, data fusion, fusion processing, intelligence reporting.

TERPES operational support—

- Translates machine-readable, airborne-collected digital data into man- and machine-readable reports (e.g., paper, magnetic tape, secure voice, plots, overlays).

- Receives and processes EA-6B mission tapes.

- Accepts, correlates, and identifies electronic emitter data from semiautomatic or automatic collection systems using various electronic parameter databases and various analysis techniques.

- Provides tactical jamming analysis.

The TERPES intelligence analysis application enables the operator to analyze
ELINT data combined with additional modernized integrated database
intelligence data to—

- Respond to intelligence requirements.
- Prepare intelligence database updates.
- Analyze threat and tactical situations.
- Estimate changes in the threat's tactical situation.

The modernized integrated database is the primary intelligence database
for intelligence analysis application operator queries and provides data fusion
capabilities. In addition to EA-6B aircraft mission tapes, the following
inputs may also be fused to maximize the support provided to tactical
intelligence operations:

- Naval intelligence database, which contains characteristics and performance
  data for weapons, sensors, and platforms.
- Electronic warfare database support, which is similar to the naval intelligence
  database and provides EA-6B tailored data.
- ELINT parameters list, which is the NSA's observed radar parametric data.
- Electronic warfare integrated reprogramming, which combines assessed
  technical radar parameters from the US Air Force EW Science and Technology
  database with the observed parameters of the NSA database.
- JSC, which is used to derive friendly electronic order of battle and radar
  parametric data.

Fusion processing is enabled by the TERPES fusion processor (TFP) and the
TERPES ELINT preprocessor. The TFP processes intelligence data from tactical
ELINT reports, sensor reports, tactical reports, and imagery intelligence reports.
The TFP provides filtering, characteristic and performance identification, order
of battle identification, technical analysis, multisource correlation, and candidate
updates; and it presents the information in various forms for analysis. One TFP-
integrated information source is the Tactical Related Applications Processor Data
Dissemination System broadcast. This broadcast is accessed using the
commander's tactical terminal and provides near real time, national-level reports
to the TERPES. This broadcast also assists the TFP in maintaining an ELINT
parameter database to track airborne, shipboard, and land-based targets. This data
can be used to develop electronic orders of battle and to perform comparative
studies on radar parameters. The TERPES ELINT preprocessor processes all
EA-6B signals of interest collected from recorder or reproducer set tape or disk

files. Specifically, the application allows for the near real time analysis of technical ELINT data. Position reports and specific unit identification and location information are used to update the TERPES database and to prepare tactical ELINT reports. TERPES also provides tactical jamming system analysis for the EA-6B aircrew and maintenance personnel. Tactical jamming system analysis consists of recovering recorded data for verifying jammed calibration, jammer on and off times, and frequency and azimuth coverage. TERPES will use mission data in the generation of EW mission summary reports.

After-fusion processing intelligence reports are generated and the primary intelligence reporting output from TERPES is in the form of post-mission reports. Post-mission reports are provided in response to established intelligence requirements. See United States Signal Intelligence Directive (USSID) 340, *Tactical ELINT Reporting*, for the most commonly used reporting formats. Other report forms may include the following reports:

- Tactical reports provide information on immediate threat activity.

- ELINT summary reports provide a summary of ELINT activity over established periods (normally 24 hours). See USSID 200, *Technical SIGINT Reporting*, for format and content.

- ELINT technical reports provide for analyst exchange of information of parametric data. See USSID 341, *Technical ELINT Reporting*, for format and content.

- Over the horizon (OTH) "GOLD" reports provide information derived from contact reports of ELINT parametrics.

- Order of battle reports provide order of battle information such as basic encyclopedia number, equipment, and location.

CHAPTER 6

External Support Activities

MAGTF EW planners use external organizations to plan and integrate electronic warfare. Support from these organizations may include personnel augmentation, functional area expertise, technical support, and planning support.

JOINT INFORMATION OPERATIONS CENTER

The Joint Information Operations Center (JIOC) was originally activated as the Joint Electronic Warfare Command, redesignated as the Joint Command and Control Warfare Center in October 1994, and renamed the JIOC in September 1999. The JIOC is located in San Antonio, TX. It is a valuable resource for the combatant commander's of unified commands and JTFs. The JIOC dispatches tailored teams to augment these staffs and provides IO expertise in all joint exercises and contingency operations. The JIOC also has EW reprogramming oversight responsibilities for the joint staff, which includes organizing, managing, and exercising joint aspects of EW reprogramming and facilitating the exchange of data used in joint EW reprogramming. Actual reprogramming of equipment, however, is a Service responsibility.

JOINT SPECTRUM CENTER

The JSC was activated in September 1994 under the direction of the joint staff's J6. The JSC assumed all the missions and responsibilities previously performed by the Electromagnetic Compatibility Center and also received additional responsibilities. Personnel in the JSC are experts in spectrum planning, electromagnetic compatibility and vulnerability, electromagnetic environmental effects, information systems, modeling and simulation, operations support, and system acquisition. The JSC provides complete, spectrum-related services to combatant commanders, military Services, and other government organizations. The JSC deploys teams in support of the combatant commanders and serves as the DOD focal point for supporting spectrum supremacy aspects of information warfare. It assists warfighters in developing and managing the JRFL and assists in the resolution of operational interference and jamming incidents. The JSC can provide databases of friendly force command and control systems for use in planning electronic protection.

JOINT WARFARE ANALYSIS CENTER

The Joint Warfare Analysis Center (JWAC) is a Navy-sponsored joint command under the Director of Operations (J3), Joint Staff. It was officially established in May 1994 and is located in Dahlgren, VA. The JWAC is instrumental in assisting the Chairman of the Joint Chiefs of Staff and commanders of unified commands in preparation and analysis of joint operational plans. It provides analysis of engineering and scientific data and integrates operational analysis with intelligence.

NATIONAL SECURITY AGENCY

The Director, NSA is the principal SIGINT and information security advisor to the Secretary of Defense, Director of the Central Intelligence Agency, and the Chairman of the Joint Chiefs of Staff. The NSA executes the information security responsibilities of the Secretary of Defense, provides SIGINT support to combatant commanders and others in accordance with their expressed formal requirements, and provides JRFL input to JFMO to ensure maximum protection from friendly interference or electronic warfare against vital SIGINT targets.

JOINT COMSEC MONITORING ACTIVITY

The Joint Communications Security Monitoring Activity (JCMA) was created in 1993 by a memorandum of agreement between the Services' operations deputies, Directors of the Joint Staff, and the NSA. The JCMA is charged with conducting COMSEC monitoring (collection, analysis, and reporting) of DOD telecommunications and automated information systems and the monitoring of related noncommunications signals. Its purpose is to identify potentially exploitable vulnerabilities and to recommend countermeasures and corrective actions. The JCMA supports real world operations, joint exercises, and DOD systems monitoring.

DEFENSE INFORMATION SYSTEMS AGENCY

The Defense Information Systems Agency (DISA) is a combat support agency responsible for the planning, development, fielding, operating, and support of command, control, communications, and information systems that serve the needs of the President, the Secretary of Defense, the Joint Chiefs of Staff, the combatant commanders, and other DOD components during both peace and war. DISA also operates the Vulnerability Analysis and Assessment Program that specifically focuses on automated information systems.

MARINE CORPS INFORMATION TECHNOLOGY AND NETWORK OPERATIONS CENTER

The Marine Corps Information Technology and Network Operations Center (MITNOC) was formed in July 1999 by merging two Marine Corps organizations: USMC Network Operations Center and Marine Corps Computers and Telecommunications Activity. The MITNOC provides support for information assurance, network operations, computer network defense, deployed support, and network security. It includes a deployed support section that provides network technical advice and assistance during the planning phase of a deployment/exercise and coordinates solutions to networking problems during the execution phase of an operation. The MITNOC also includes a Marine computer emergency response team that offers 24-hour technical response to computer security incidents.

NAVAL AIR WARFARE CENTER WEAPONS DIVISION

Naval Air Warfare Center Weapons Division's (NAWCWD's) EA-6B EA lab develops and tests radar receivers/jammers, communications receivers/jammers, satellite communications systems, datalinks, and threat databases. It continuously improves the EA-6B through upgrades to its operational flight programs and also provides support to engineering upgrades of its weapons capabilities.

NAWCWD works in conjunction with the Navy-Marine Corps Electronic Warfare Reprogrammable Library Support Program at the Fleet Information Warfare Center to address electronic warfare reprogramming issues. The Fleet Information Warfare Center is designated as the Navy's functional database manager for information warfare per Office of the Chief of Naval Operations Instruction (OPNAVINST) 3430.23, *Tactical Electronic Warfare Reprogrammable Library (EWRL) Support Program.*

APPENDIX A

Joint Electronic Warfare Reports

Joint publications set forth approved procedures and formats for standardizing EW message traffic in joint operations. This material in this appendix was extracted from CJCSM 6120.05, *Manual for Tactical Command and Control Planning Guidance for Joint Operations: Joint Interface Operational Procedures for Message Text Formats.*

EW Mission Summary (EWMSNSUM)

a. <u>PURPOSE</u>. The EWMSNSUM is used to summarize significant EW missions and the status of offensive EW assets. The EWMSNSUM will not be used to report the results of ES operations. The TACREP will be used to report ES operational results.

b. <u>ORIGINATOR</u>. TOC, AOC, MAGTF COC.

c. <u>ADDRESSEE</u>. JOC (record only), TOC, AOC, MAGTF COC.

d. <u>METHOD OF TRANSMISSION</u>. When EWMSNSUM is sent to the JOC, it is sent by record only. When sent cross-Service, the primary method of transmission is record with voice as an alternate. The message preparer may use any one or all of the formatted sets when reporting the EW summary activity.

e. <u>FREQUENCY OF TRANSMISSION/UPDATE</u>. As required, as specified in COMJTF OPLAN, or in accordance with established OPLANS for the theater of operations.

f. <u>PROCEDURES</u>. The EWMSNSUM is used by all EW- and EA-capable surface and air units to provide information on EW operations. It is used by the Service component commander to report significant events for subsequent analysis.

Electronic Warfare Employment Message (EWEM)

a. PURPOSE. The EWEM is used to provide the COMJTF with the component commander's intentions for the employment of EA for either a specific reporting period or for a specific EW mission. Reporting requirements are to be established by the COMJTF. The EWEM is used by the JOC to eliminate potential EW mission conflicts. It may also be used by component commanders to warn or notify of intended EA actions.

b. ORIGINATOR. TOC, EWC, OTC/CWC/CATF, AOC, MAGTF COC, AFSOD.

c. ADDRESSEE. JOC, TOC, AAWC, ASWC, ASUWC, EWC, OTC/CWC/ CATF, AOC, MAGTF COC, JOC(SOC/JSOTF), NSWTG, SFOB.

d. METHOD OF TRANSMISSION. The primary method of transmission is record with voice as an alternate.

e. FREQUENCY OF TRANSMISSION/UPDATE. As established by the COMJTF OPLAN, as required to reflect a Service component's EW intentions, or as required to respond to an EWRTM.

f. PROCEDURES. The EWEM can simply reflect a Service component commander's intentions for the employment of EA; but as the required response to an EWRTM, the EWEM also contains the Service component's planned EW support.

Electronic Warfare Approval Message (EWAM)

a. <u>PURPOSE</u>. The EWAM is used by the COMJTF to approve or modify the total joint operations EW plan.

b. <u>ORIGINATOR</u>. JOC.

c. <u>ADDRESSEE</u>. TOC, AAWC, ASWC, ASUWC, EWC, OTC/CWC/CATF, AOC, MAGTF COC.

d. <u>METHOD OF TRANSMISSION</u>. The primary method of transmission is record with voice as an alternate.

e. <u>FREQUENCY OF TRANSMISSION/UPDATE</u>. As required.

f. <u>PROCEDURES</u>. The COMJTF references the Service component's message, identifies the applicable timeframe, and approves, disapproves, or modifies EW tasking. If disapproved or modification is directed, amplifying details are forwarded. When no conflicts exist in the component commander's EW schedule and the overall EW plan satisfies joint mission objectives, the EWAM will simply state "approved." If changes, cancellations, or modifications to the joint operations EW plan are required, the JOC will so state and send the EWAM to the appropriate Service component. The Service component's schedule will be adjusted as directed through the normal tasking cycle. Blanket EA restrictions (such as jam-free frequencies) will be provided via the ORDER or PLANORDCHG message. Control measures (such as "stop EA") will be handled by standard voice procedures and not by this message.

Tactical Report (TACREP)

a. PURPOSE. The TACREP is used only to provide perishable information of tactical significance, for the immediate attention of the tactical commander.

b. ORIGINATOR. JIC (JTF), ASAC, AAWC, ASWC, ASWOC, ASUWC, EWC, FOSIC, OTC/CWC/CATF, SUBOPCONCEN, E-3, DSU/(AF), AOC-INTEL, WOC-F, RADBN DET, MAGTF-INTEL, JOC (SOC/JSOTF), AFSOD, AFSOE, FOB, NSWTG, NSWTU, SFOB.

c. ADDRESSEE. JIC (JTF), DIA, ASAC, AAWC, ASWC, ASWOC, ASUWC, EWC, FCC, FOSIC, OTC/CWC/CATF, SUBOPCONCEN, AME, DSU(AF), E-3, AOC-INTEL, WOC-F, RADBN DET, MAGTF-INTEL, JOC (SOC/JSOTF), AFSOD, AFSOE, FOB, NSWTG, NSWTU, SFOB.

d. METHOD OF TRANSMISSION. The primary method of transmission is record with voice as alternate. GENSER or SCI channels are used as appropriate. The TACREP is normally sent with an immediate or flash precedence because of the high-priority and perishable nature of the information.

e. FREQUENCY OF TRANSMISSION/UPDATE. As required.

f. COMMENTS. The TACREP is used to alert commanders of immediate threats to friendly forces. Amplifying information may be reported by other message formats (e.g., INTREP, SIREP). Because of the significance of this report, the message should not be delayed to obtain all possible data on a continuing event. For maritime operations reporting, the TACREP is used to report contacts developed by HFDF assets.

Note: Since the TACREP is the primary MTF used for reporting time-critical intelligence information, it can be sent by any C2/IE element in addition to those identified in subparagraph b above.

Electronic Warfare Requesting/Tasking Message (EWRTM)

a. <u>PURPOSE</u>. The EWRTM is used by the COMJTF to task component commanders to perform EW operations in support of the overall joint EW plan and to support component EW operations, and also used by component commanders to request EW support from sources outside their command.

b. <u>ORIGINATOR</u>. JOC, TOC, EWC, OTC/CWC/CATF, AOC, MAGTF COC, JOC (SOC/JSOTF).

c. <u>ADDRESSEE</u>. JOC, TOC, AAWC, ASWC, ASUWC, EWC, FOSIC, OTC/ CWC/CATF, AOC, MAGTF COC, AFSOD.

d. <u>METHOD OF TRANSMISSION</u>. The primary method of transmission is record with voice as an alternate.

e. <u>FREQUENCY OF TRANSMISSION/UPDATE</u>. As required.

f. <u>PROCEDURES</u>. The EWRTM will not be used to request or task support from SIGINT assets. Mission coordination details and additional specific equipment parameters will be exchanged using messages such as the SIEPCM. Requesting numbering will be in accordance with JTF OPLANs or OPORDs. The COMJTF's tasking or Service component commanders's request (EWRTM) will be responded to by the Electronic Warfare Employment Message (EWEM).

Tactical ELINT Report (TACELINT)

a. PURPOSE. The TACELINT is used to report time-critical operational ELINT and parametric information. Information contained therein may be used for indications and warnings, data base maintenance, orders of battle, and strike planning. ELINT collectors use this message format as a reporting vehicle. The COMJTF uses this message format to advise the joint force of updates to the ELINT order of battle or data base.

b. ORIGINATOR. JIC(JTF), AAWC, ASWC, ASUWC, EWC, FOSIC, OTC/CWC/ CATF, II(AF), TEP, RADBN DET, MAGTF-INTEL, TERPES.

c. ADDRESSEE. JIC(JTF), DIA, ASAC, AAWC, ASWC, ASWOC, ASUWC, EWC, FCC, FOSIC, OTC/CWC/CATF, SUBOPCONCEN, DSU(AF), AOC-INTEL, RADBN DET, MAGTF-INTEL, TERPES.

d. METHOD OF TRANSMISSION. The primary method of transmission is record. Voice transmission is a backup for ASAC, JIC interfaces and the SCI-capable C2/IE elements. GENSER or SCI channels are used as appropriate. The voice message may also be used as a RACKET (initial contact), RENT (parameter report), or TROUT (triangulation) report, depending on the lines used.

e. FREQUENCY OF TRANSMISSION/UPDATE. As required.

f. COMMENTS. The TACELINT report advises joint forces of changes and updates to the ground, naval, and electronics orders of battle (EOB). This message will be prepared whenever vital information is obtained. The COMJTF may designate an internal or external organization to maintain the JTF ELINT data base. This will be published in the JTF letters of instruction and/or OPLANs, and the designated organization will be an information addressee on all ELINT message traffic. Any information with less that 95 percent confidence factor must be amplified in an appropriate free-text set.

EA Data Message (EADAT)

a. <u>PURPOSE</u>. The EADAT is used to report EA strobe data in the absence of a TADIL A or TADIL B link.

b. <u>ORIGINATOR</u>. ADACP, AAWC, OTC/CWC/CATF, CRC/CRP, DSU(AF), E-3, TACC/TADC(M), TAOC.

c. <u>ADDRESSEE</u>. ADACP, AAWC, OTC/CWC/CATF, CRC/CRP, DSU(AF), E-3, TACC/TADC(M), TAOC, ABCCC.

d. <u>METHOD OF TRANSMISSION</u>. Voice only.

e. <u>FREQUENCY OF TRANSMISSION/UPDATE</u>. As required to report an EA signal. Update every 5 minutes until location of jamming has been determined.

f. <u>COMMENTS</u>. This message is used to report an EA strobe from an affected or detecting unit's position to an aircraft emitting EA. It is used to determine the location of a hostile or unknown aircraft emitting EA. It is reported by the detecting unit to all units on a net when the data link is degraded or not operational. After receipt of several EADAT messages, it is possible to determine the source of enemy EA by comparing lines of bearing from the different origins (triangulation). Once this is accomplished, the EA aircraft can be engaged with friendly interceptors or SAMs. Requirements for the EADAT terminates when the EA source is destroyed, the EA ceases or the TADIL reporting is restored. As soon as the tactical situation allows, a MIJIFEEDER report should be submitted.

SIGINT/EA Planning/Coordinating Message (SIEPCM)

a. PURPOSE. The SIEPCM is used to plan and coordinate SIGINT collection and EA communications or noncommunications missions. It is also a vehicle for requesting cross-Service assets to satisfy tasks beyond a component Service's capabilities.

b. ORIGINATOR. JIC(JTF), ASAC, ASWC, ASUWC, EWC, FOSIC, OTC/CWC/ CATF, DSU(AF), RADBN DET.

c. ADDRESSEE. JIC(JTF), DIA, ASAC, AWUWC, EWC, OTC/CWC/CATF, DSU(AF), RADBN DET.

d. METHOD OF TRANSMISSION. Record only; SCI only.

e. FREQUENCY OF TRANSMISSION/UPDATE. As required.

f. COMMENTS. Service component planners will use this message to resolve and/or preclude EA/EP mutual interference problems and to maximize SIGINT/EA resource coverage within the JTF's AOR. The JTF headquarters will incorporate the information from this message into the planning process. Each Service component's request for assistance beyond their capability will be sent to the COMJTF and requires justification. Unless otherwise directed, the SIEPCMs or MSGCORRCANXs submitted subsequent to the initial message will normally report only modification to the previous SIEPCM.

g. PROCEDURES. The SIEPCM is used to request and/or coordinate cross-Service EA/SIGINT information. If the C2/IE element (supporting) that receives the SIEPCM needs more COMINT support, it sends a COMINTADTSK message to the appropriate facility. The recipient of the COMINTADTSK sends a MSGCORRCANX to the SIEPCM what indicates acceptance of the COMINTADTSK. If the recipient for the COMINTADTSK is unable to accept the tasking, he sends an RRI to inform the JIC(JTF). If COMINT coverage assistance is requested (without a SIEPCM), the tasking unit sends a COMINTADTSK to the appropriate tasked unit. If the tasked unit accepts the task, he sends an RRI to the tasking Service component. If the tasked Service component is unable to accept the tasking, he sends an RRI to the tasking Service component and the JIC(JTF).

ELINT Requirement Tasking Message (ERTM)

a. <u>PURPOSE</u>. The ERTM is used by operational commanders to task resources under their OPCON for the purpose of ELINT collection, or to request ELINT collection from sources outside of their OPCON.

b. <u>ORIGINATOR</u>. JIC(JTF), ASAC, DSU(AF), AOC-INTEL, RADBN DET, MAGTF-INTEL, TERPES.

c. <u>ADDRESSEE</u>. JIC(JTF), DIA, ASAC, EWC, OTC/CWC/CATF, DSU(AF), AOC-INTEL, RADBN DET, MAGTF-INTEL, TERPES.

d. <u>METHOD OF TRANSMISSION</u>. Record only. Transmission channels are GENSER or SCI as appropriate.

e. <u>FREQUENCY OF TRANSMISSION/UPDATE</u>. As required.

f. <u>COMMENTS</u>. Component commanders submit the ERTM to the COMJTF (JIC(JTF)) when requesting ELINT collection outside their OPCON. If the COMJTF approves the request, COMJTF (JIC(JTF)) will submit an ERTM to the appropriate source internal or external to the joint force.

g. <u>PROCEDURES</u>. The ERTM can be used by operational commanders to task resources under their OPCON or request ELINT collection from sources outside their OPCON. If the resources are under the OPCON of the Service component or JIC(JTF), the Service component or JIC(JTF) sends an ERTM to the supporting Service component. If the supporting Service component accepts the tasking, the supporting Service component will perform the mission and send a TACELINT message to the tasking Service component. If the supporting Service component does not accept the tasking, the supporting Service component sends an RRI message to the tasking Service component. If the resources are outside the OPCON of the tasking Service component, the tasking Service component becomes the requesting Service component and sends an ERTM to the JIC(JTF) for support. If the JIC(JTF) approves the request, the JIC(JTF) sends the ERTM to the supporting Service component. The supporting Service component will then send a TACELINT or TACREP, depending on the request, to the requesting Service component with the JIC(JTF) as an information addressee.

Air Support Request (AIRSUPREQ)

a. PURPOSE. The AIRSUPREQ is used to request preplanned and immediate close air support, interdiction, reconnaissance, surveillance, escort, helicopter airlift, and other aircraft missions.

b. ORIGINATOR. TOC, ASAC, ASWC, OTC/CWC/CATF, ABCCC, AOC, DASC, TACC/TADC(M), JOC(SOC/JSOTF), AFSOD, AFSOE, FOB, NSWTG, NSWTU, SFOB.

c. ADDRESSEE. JFACC (if desired), JOC, FCC, OTC/CWC/CATF, ASOC, ABCCC, AOC, DASC, MAGTF COC, TACC/TADC (M), JOC(SOC/JSOTF).

d. METHOD OF TRANSMISSION. The primary method of transmission is record with voice as alternate; however, the best and most effective method of transmission should be based on the condition of the communications system. The voice message formats are normally used for immediate requests when the time-on-target is less than 6 hours from the time of the request. COMJTF MAY DESIGNATE THE DD-1972 (NON-JNTACCS) FORMAT BE USED IN PLACE OF THE AIRSUPREQ VOICE FORMATS.

e. FREQUENCY OF TRANSMISSION/UPDATE

(1) PREPLANNED. The AIRSUPREQ must be submitted in time to the supporting Service component so each Service component is able to include the request in its daily ALLOREQ to the JFACC (if designated). Each Service component must specify a not later than deadline for daily receipt of AIRSUPREQs. If additional information becomes available on an approved request, the requesting Service component may pass the information to the tasked Service component using an AIRSUPREQ message.

CAUTION: The intent of the AIRSUPREQ to be submitted not later than deadline for inclusion into the ALLOREQ during the air tasking cycle for preplanned mission requests must be clearly understood. The intent is not to force battalions or squadrons to submit AIRSUPREQs more than 24 hours in advance. The intent is for the knowledgeable echelon to plan, coordinate, and request those detailed air missions they require in order to accomplish their missions during an air tasking day. AIRSUPREQs submitted as preplanned mission requests are usually planned AND REQUESTED by a division or wing or higher echelon planning staffs based upon the information they know at the time. A battalion or squadron, except in unusual circumstances, will not be aware of the changing tactical situation sufficiently in advance to provide air missions details for preplanned AIRSUPREQs. APPROPRIATE PLANNING AND REQUESTING

MUST BE DONE BY THE ECHELON AWARE OF THE NEED FOR AN AIR MISSION. If a battalion is aware, it should submit the AIRSUPREQ; if however, only the division is aware, it must submit the AIRSUPREQ.

(2) IMMEDIATE. As required to request immediate air support. The AIRSUPREQ is transmitted when an unexpected requirement is brought about by a changing tactical situation. The AIRSUPREQ is updated as necessary to provide additional, essential mission details.

f. COMMENTS. The AIRSUPREQ can be used to request air support directly from the other Service components, if authorized, or from other Service components through the JOC/JFACC (if designated). NOTE: The AIRSUPREQ does not apply to SAR and fixed-wing aircraft missions.

g. PROCEDURES. The AIRSUPREQ is used in the air tasking cycle; i.e., it is not a stand-alone message. For preplanned mission requests, the JOC/JFACC (if designated) should be an information addressee on all record AIRSUPREQ messages.

(1) When an Amphibious Force (AF) is formed, the CLF will make immediate air requests by submitting the AIRSUPREQ to the CATF. The CATF will respond with the REQCONF message. If the CATF is unable to support the request, the CLF or CATF (depending on the Service agreements) then submits the request to the JOC/JFACC (if designated).

(2) The following voice only messages are used as a backup for the AIRSUPREQ record MTF message for preplanned air support.

(a) Air Request Support (AIRREQSUP). This voice only message is used to request preplanned air support for escort, lift, and other missions. It is not to be used for fixed-wing airlift; for fixed-wing airlift use the AIRLIFTREQ message.

(b) Air Request Jammer (AIRREQJAM). This voice only message is used to request preplanned and immediate EW air support missions.

(c) Air Request Reconnaissance (AIRREQRECON). This voice only message is used to request preplanned and immediate aerial reconnaissance support missions.

Air Request Jammer (AIRREQJAM)

a. PURPOSE. The AIRREQJAM is used to request preplanned and immediate EW air support missions. This message is transmitted by voice only.

b. ORIGINATOR. ASAC, TOC, ASWC, OTC/CWC/CATF, ABCCC, AOC, DASC, TACC/TADC (M).

c. ADDRESSEE. JFACC (if designated), JOC, TOC, FCC, OTC/CWC/CATF, ASOC, ABCCC, AOC, DASC, TACC/TADC (M).

d. METHOD OF TRANSMISSION. Voice only; it is a backup to the AIRSUPREQ record message.

e. FREQUENCY OF TRANSMISSION/UPDATE. As required.

f. COMMENTS. The message is used as a backup means to the AIRSUPREQ record message for preplanned and immediate air support, or when timely dissemination of information precludes record message formatting.

Electronic Warfare Frequency
Deconfliction Message (EWDECONFLICT)

a. <u>PURPOSE</u>. The EWDECONFLICT is used to promulgate a list of protected, guarded, and taboo frequencies so as to ensure friendly force use of the frequency spectrum without adverse impact from friendly EA.

b. <u>ORIGINATOR</u>. JOC.

c. <u>ADDRESSEE</u>. TOC, OTC/CWC/CATF, AOC, MAGTF COC.

d. <u>METHOD OF TRANSMISSION</u>. Primary is record with voice as an alternate. Transmission channels are GENSER or SCI as appropriate.

e. <u>FREQUENCY OF TRANSMISSION/UPDATE</u>. The Joint Restricted Frequency List (JRFL) is constantly being modified and a EWDECONFLICT is needed (at least daily) to protect frequencies from being jammed or other forms of manipulation.

f. <u>COMMENTS</u>. The EWDECONFLICT message provides a rapid and efficient means to promulgate the JRFL. The JRFL is the only authorized mechanism through which the Department of Defense can protect frequencies from jamming, or other forms of manipulation.

Meaconing, Intrusion, Jamming, and
Interference Feeder Report (MIJIFEEDER)

a. <u>PURPOSE</u>. The MIJIFEEDER is used as a primary means of sharing MIJI incidents in a timely manner, and provides for joint exchange of tactical MIJI information, including electro-optic interference.

b. <u>ORIGINATOR</u>. JIC(JTF), AAWC, ASWC, ASWOC, ASUWC, EWC, FOSIC, OTC/CWC/CATF, AOC-INTEL, WOC-F, WOC-R, WOC-A, RADBN DET, MAGTF-INTEL, TERPES, JOC(SOC/JSOTF), AFSOD, AFSOE, FOB, NSWTG, NSWTU, SFOB.

c. <u>ADDRESSEE</u>. JIC(JTF), DIA, ASAC, AAWC, ASWC, ASWOC, ASUWC, EWC, FCC, FOSIC, OTC/CWC/CATF, SUBOPCONCEN, AME, AOC-INTEL, WOC-F, WOC-R, WOC-A, RADBN DET, TERPES, MAGTF-INTEL, JOC(SOC/JSOTF), AFSOD, AFSOE, FOB, NSWTG, NSWTU, SFOB.

d. <u>METHOD OF TRANSMISSION</u>. Primary method of transmission is record with voice as alternate; GENSER.

e. <u>FREQUENCY OF TRANSMISSION/UPDATE</u>. As soon as any MIJI incident occurs. Use "IMMEDIATE" precedence.

f. <u>COMMENTS</u>. A MIJIFEEDER message should be sent even when in doubt about any unknown interference. A MIJIFEEDER can help resolve friendly mutual interference. The COMJTF will coordinate if the reported MIJI incident was caused by external sources, the COMJTF will report the incident in accordance with Reporting MIJI of Electromagnetic Systems, RCS: JCS-1066, AR 105-3, OPNAVINST 3430.18, and MCO 3430.3. The MIJIFEEDER can be transmitted or received by any C2/IE element in addition to those listed in paragraphs b and c above. Any C2/IE element encountering MIJI must submit a MIJIFEEDER

Sensitive Information Report (SIREP)

a. <u>PURPOSE</u>. The SIREP is used to provide sensitive information on events or conditions that may have a significant impact on current planning of an operation, but of less time criticality than a TACREP. This message provides a sensitive file maintenance update mechanism.

b. <u>ORIGINATOR</u>. JIC(JTF), DIA, ASAC, DSU(AF), RADBN DET.

c. <u>ADDRESSEE</u>. JIC(JTF), DIA, ASAC, AAWC, ASWOC, FCC, FOSIC, OTC/ CWC/CATF, SUBOPCONCEN, DSU(AF), RADBN DET.

d. <u>METHOD OF TRANSMISSION</u>. Record; SCI only.

e. <u>FREQUENCY OF TRANSMISSION/UPDATE</u>. As required.

f. <u>COMMENTS</u>. The SIREP may be used to supplement information disseminated in other reports; e.g. TACREP, ITREP. When used in this capacity, the reference set of the SIREP must identify the original message. A SIREP reports information that affects planning rather than execution actions. The SIREP may also be a feeder report for the SISUM. The SIREP is transmitted for SCI-capable units to higher, lower, and lateral C2/IE elements.

Stop Jamming Message (STOP JAMMING)

a. <u>PURPOSE</u>. The STOP JAMMING message is used to terminate a jamming task being conducted by an EA asset.

b. <u>ORIGINATOR</u>. Any established C2/IE element.

c. <u>ADDRESSEE</u>. Next higher headquarters and any established C2/IE element, specifically the C2/IE element (unit or facility) that might be affected by disruption of tactical communications.

d. <u>METHOD OF TRANSMISSION</u>. Record, voice backup. GENSER. Voice may become primary if record means has been disrupted.

e. <u>COMMENTS</u>. The STOP JAMMING message is used by the COMJTF to stop friendly jamming operations, when those operations are affecting the joint information flow. It is used by any C2/IE element to request termination of friendly jamming operations which are affecting their information flow. The use of this message DOES NOT relieve the originator from the requirements of submitting a MIJIFEEDER report.

APPENDIX B

Electronic Warfare Tab Format

Copy no. ___ of ___ copies
OFFICIAL DESIGNATION OF COMMAND
PLACE OF ISSUE
Date/time group
Message reference number

TAB B TO APPENDIX 3 TO ANNEX C TO OPERATION PLAN (Number)
(Operation CODEWORD) (U)

ELECTRONIC WARFARE

(U) REFERENCES: List basic documents required.

1. (U) Situation

   a. (U) Enemy. Refer to annex B. Provide an estimate of the enemy's
   command, control, communications, noncommunications (e.g., radar), and
   EW systems, capabilities, limitations, and vulnerabilities. Identify the
   enemy's ability to interfere with the accomplishment of the EW mission.

   b. (U) Friendly. Provide a summary of friendly EW facilities, resources, and
   organizations that may affect EW planning by subordinate commanders.
   Identify the friendly foreign forces with which subordinate commanders
   may operate.

   c. (U) Civilian and/or Neutral Facilities. Identify the civilian and/or neutral
   facilities, resources, and organizations that may affect EW planning.
   Determine potential collateral effects.

CLASSIFICATION

d. (U) <u>Assumptions</u>. State any significant assumptions concerning friendly or enemy capabilities and COAs that significantly influence the planning of EW operations.

2. (U) <u>Mission</u>. Provide a concise statement that describes the EW mission and how EW operations will support the mission in the basic plan.

3. (U) <u>Execution</u>

a. (U) <u>Commander's Intent</u>. Describe the role of electronic warfare in the commander's IO strategy.

b. (U) <u>Concept of Operations</u>. Summarize the scope of EW operations and the methods and resources to be employed. Identify the employment of both organic and nonorganic capabilities. Identify how electronic warfare will support the other elements of IO and SEAD.

c. (U) <u>Tasks</u>. Use separate, numbered subparagraphs to assign individual EW tasks and responsibilities to each component or element of the joint force or MAGTF. Include all instructions that are unique to the specific component or element.

d. (U) <u>Coordinating Instructions</u>

(1) (U) Provide instructions that may be applicable to two or more components or elements.

(2) (U) Include support instructions for other types of operations (e.g., deception, unconventional warfare, psychological operations, SIGINT).

(3) (U) Provide emission control guidance (place lengthy or detailed guidance in an exhibit to this tab).

(4) (U) Coordinate with the G-6/S-6 to generate the RFL.

(5) (U) State or refer to policies, doctrine, and procedures that provide guidelines to be followed in order to implement this plan. Establish any additional guidance to be followed, as well as authorized deviations from standard practices. Identify and describe any EW constraints that apply to the operations.

CLASSIFICATION

CLASSIFICATION

6) (U) Provide guidance on the employment of each activity, special measure, or procedure that is to be used but is not covered in Annex C.

4. (U) Administration and Logistics

   a. (U) Administration. Include necessary administrative guidance.

   (1) (U) Provide guidance when modifications to Service electromagnetic interference reporting instructions are necessary.

   (2) (U) Identify required reports (include examples).

   b. (U) Logistics. Provide special instructions pertaining to logistic support of EW operations.

5. (U) Command and Signals

   a. (U) Command. Designate the lead EW activity.

   b. (U) Signals. Identify any special or unusual EW-related communications requirements.

   c. (U) After-Action Reports. Identify the requirements for after-action reporting.

CLASSIFICATION

APPENDIX C

Glossary

Section I. Acronyms

ACE	aviation combat element
AIRREQJAM	air request jammer
AIRSUPREQ	air support request
AJP	allied joint publication
C4	command, control, communications, and computers
CJCSI	Chairman of the Joint Chiefs of Staff Instruction
CJCSM	Chairman of the Joint Chiefs of Staff Manual
COA	course of action
COMSEC	communications security
DISA	Defense Information Systems Agency
DOD	Department of Defense
EA	electronic attack
EADAT	electronic data message
ELINT	electronic intelligence
EMCON	emission control
EP	electronic protection
ERTM	ELINT requirement tasking message
ES	electronic warfare support
EW	electronic warfare
EWAM	electronic warfare approval
EWCC	electronic warfare coordination cell
EWDECONFLICT	electronic warfare frequency deconfliction message
EWEM	electronic warfare employment message
EWMSNSUM	EW mission summary
EWO	electronic warfare officer
EWRTM	electronic warfare requesting/tasking message
HARM	high-speed antiradiation missile
IO	information operations
JCEWS	joint force commander's electronic warfare staff

JCMA . . . . joint communications security monitoring activity
JFACC. . . . . joint force air component commander
JFC . . . . joint force commander
JFMO. . . . . joint frequency management office
JIC. . . . . .joint intelligence center
JIOC . . . . .joint information operations center
JOC . . . . .joint operations center
JP . . . . joint publications
JRFL . . . . joint restricted frequency list
JSC . . . . .Joint Spectrum Center
J-SEAD . . . . .joint suppression of enemy air defenses
JTCB. . . . . .joint targeting coordination board
JTF. . . . . joint task force
JWAC . . . . .joint warfare analysis center
MAGTF . . . . Marine air-ground task force
MC. . . . . military committee
MCPP . . . . Marine Corps Planning Process
MCWP . . . . Marine Corps warfighting publication
MEF. . . . . .Marine expeditionary force
MEWSS. . . . . mobile electronic warfare support system
MIJIFEEDER . . . . Meaconing, Intrusion, Jamming, and Interference Feeder Report
MITNOC. . . . . Marine Corps Information Technology and Network Operations Center
MNF . . . . multinational force
NATO . . . . North Atlantic Treaty Organization
NAWCWD . . . . .Naval Air Warfare Center Weapons Division
NSA. . . . . .National Security Agency
OCAC. . . . . operations control and analysis center
OPLAN . . . . operation plan
OPNAVINST. . . . . Office of the Chief of Naval Operations Instruction
OPORD . . . . operation order
OPSEC . . . . operations security
OTH. . . . . over the horizon
PIP. . . . . product improvement program
RadBn . . . . .radio battalion
RFL . . . . .restricted frequency list
ROE. . . . . rules of engagement
SEAD . . . . suppression of enemy air defenses

SIEPCM .SIGINT/EA planning/coordinating message
SIGINT. . . . . signals intelligence
SIREP. . . . . .sensitive information report
SSU. . . . . signals intelligence support unit
STANAG . . . . .standardization agreement
STOP JAMMING. . . . . .stop jamming message
TACELINT. . . . . tactical ELINT report
TACREP. . . . . .tactical report
TEAMS . . . . .tactical EA-6B mission planning system
TERPES . . . . tactical electronic reconnaissance
processing and evaluation system
TFP. . . . . TERPES fusion processor
US. . . . . United States
USSID . . . . .United States Signal Intelligence Directive
VHF . . . . .very high frequency
VMAQ . . . . Marine tactical electronic warfare squadron

Section II. Definitions

battle damage assessment—The timely and accurate estimate of damage resulting from the application of military force, either lethal or non-lethal, against a predetermined objective. Battle damage assessment can be applied to the employment of all types of weapon systems (air, ground, naval, and special forces weapon systems) throughout the range of military operations. Battle damage assessment is primarily an intelligence responsibility with required inputs and coordination from the operators. Battle damage assessment is composed of physical damage assessment, functional damage assessment, and target system assessment. Also called BDA. (JP 2-0)

centers of gravity—Those characteristics, capabilities, or localities from which a military force derives its freedom of action, physical strength, or will to fight. Also called COGs. (JP 3-0)

commander, landing force—The officer designated in the order initiating the amphibious operation as the commander of the landing force for an amphibious operation. Also called CLF. (JP 3-02)

commander's critical information requirements—A comprehensive list of information requirements identified by the commander as being critical in facilitating timely information management and the decision making process that affect successful mission accomplishment. The two key subcomponents are critical friendly force information and priority intelligence requirements. Also called CCIR. (JP 5-00.2)

communications security—The protection resulting from all measures designed to deny unauthorized persons information of value that might be derived from the possession and study of telecommunications, or to mislead unauthorized persons in their interpretation of the results of such possession and study. Also called COMSEC. (JP 1-02)

directed energy—An umbrella term covering technologies that relate to the production of a beam of concentrated electromagnetic energy or atomic or subatomic particles. Also called DE. (JP 1-02)

electromagnetic deception—The deliberate radiation, reradiation, alteration, suppression, absorption, denial, enhancement, or reflection of electromagnetic energy in a manner intended to convey misleading information to an enemy or to enemy electromagnetic-dependent weapons, thereby degrading or neutralizing the enemy's combat capability. (JP 1-02)

electromagnetic jamming—The deliberate radiation, reradiation, or reflection of electromagnetic energy for the purpose of preventing or reducing an enemy's effective use of the electromagnetic spectrum, and with the intent of degrading or neutralizing the enemy's combat capability. (JP 1-02)

electronic attack—That division of electronic warfare involving the use of electromagnetic energy, directed energy, or antiradiation weapons to attack personnel, facilities, or equipment with the intent of degrading, neutralizing, or destroying enemy combat capability and is considered a form of fires. Also called EA. (Joint Pub 1-02)

electronic protection—That division of electronic warfare involving passive and active means taken to protect personnel, facilities, and equipment from any effects of friendly or enemy employment of electronic warfare that degrade, neutralize, or destroy friendly combat capability. Also called EP. (Joint Pub 3-51)

electronic warfare—Any military action involving the use of electromagnetic and directed energy to control the electromagnetic spectrum or to attack the enemy. Also called EW. (Joint Pub 3-51)

electronic warfare support—That division of electronic warfare involving actions tasked by, or under direct control of, an operational commander to search for, intercept, identify, and locate or localize sources of intentional and unintentional radiated electromagnetic energy for the purpose of immediate threat recognition, targeting, planning and conduct of future operations. Thus, electronic warfare support provides information required for decisions involving electronic warfare operations and other tactical actions such as threat avoidance, targeting, and homing. Also called ES. (Joint Pub 3-51)

emission control—The selective and controlled use of electromagnetic, acoustic, or other emitters to optimize command and control capabilities while minimizing, for operations security: a. detection by enemy sensors; b. mutual interference among friendly systems; and/or c. enemy interference with the ability to execute a military deception plan. Also called EMCON. (JP 1-02)

essential elements of friendly information—Key questions likely to be asked by adversary officials and intelligence systems about specific friendly intentions, capabilities, and activities, so they can obtain answers critical to their operational effectiveness. Also called EEFI. (JP 1-02)

guarded frequencies—Enemy frequencies that are currently being exploited for combat information and intelligence. A guarded frequency is time-oriented in that the guarded frequency list changes as the enemy assumes different combat postures. These frequencies may be jammed after the commander has weighed the potential gain against the loss of technical information. (JP 3-51)

imitative electromagnetic deception—The introduction of electromagnetic energy into enemy systems that imitates enemy emissions. (JP 1-02)

information operations—Actions taken to affect adversary information and information systems while defending one's own information and information systems. Also called IO. (JP 3-13)

information security—The protection of information and information systems against unauthorized access or modification of information, whether in storage, processing, or transit, against the denial of service to authorized users. Information security includes those measures necessary to detect, document, and counter such threats. Information security is composed of computer security and communications security. Also called INFOSEC.

joint restricted frequency list—A time and geographically-oriented listing of TABOO, PROTECTED, and GUARDED functions, nets, and frequencies. It should be limited to the number of frequencies necessary for friendly forces to accomplish objectives. Also called JRFL. (JP 3-51)

joint suppression of enemy air defenses—A broad term that includes all suppression of enemy air defense activities provided by one component of the joint force in support of another. Also called J-SEAD.

joint targeting coordination board—A group formed by the joint force commander to accomplish broad targeting oversight functions that may include but are not limited to coordinating targeting information, providing targeting guidance and priorities, and preparing and/or refining joint target lists. This board is normally comprised of representatives from the joint force staff, all components and, if required, component subordinate units. Also called JTCB. (JP 3-05.5)

joint task force—A joint force that is constituted and so designated by the Secretary of Defense, a combatant commander, a subunified commander, or an existing joint task force commander. Also called a JTF. (JP 0-2)

landing force—A Marine Corps or Army task organization formed to conduct amphibious operations. The landing force, together with the amphibious task force and other forces, constitute the amphibious force. Also called LF.

operations security—A process of identifying critical information and subsequently analyzing friendly actions attendant to military operations and other activities to: a. identify those actions that can be observed by adversary intelligence systems; b. determine indicators that hostile intelligence systems might obtain that could be interpreted or pieced together to derive critical information in time to be useful to adversaries; and c. select and execute measures that eliminate or reduce to an acceptable level the vulnerabilities of friendly actions to adversary exploitation. Also called OPSEC. (JP 3-54)

priority intelligence requirements—Those intelligence requirements for which a commander has an anticipated and stated priority in the task of planning and decision making. Also called PIRs. (JP 2-0)

psychological operations—Planned operations to convey selected information and indicators to foreign audiences to influence their emotions, motives, objective reasoning, and ultimately the behavior of foreign governments, organizations, groups, and individuals. The purpose of psychological operations is to induce or reinforce foreign attitudes and behavior favorable to the originator's objectives. Also called PSYOP. (JP 1-02)

rules of engagement—Directives issued by competent military authority that delineate the circumstances and limitations under which United States forces will initiate and/or continue combat engagement with other forces encountered. Also called ROE. (JP 1-02)

signals intelligence—1. A category of intelligence comprising either individually or in combination all communications intelligence, electronic intelligence, and foreign instrumentation signals intelligence, however transmitted. 2. Intelligence derived from communications, electronic, and foreign instrumentation signals. Also called SIGINT. (JP 2-0)

special information operations—Information operations that by their sensitive nature and due to their potential effect or impact, security requirements, or risk to the national security of the United States, require a special review and approval process. Also called SIO. (JP 3-13)

transmission security—The component of communications security that results from all measures designed to protect transmissions from interception and exploitation by means other than cryptanalysis. (JP 1-02)

wartime reserve modes—Characteristics and operating procedures of sensor, communications, navigation aids, threat recognition, weapons, and countermeasures systems that will contribute to military effectiveness if unknown to or misunderstood by opposing commanders before they are used, but could be exploited or neutralized if known in advance. Wartime reserve modes are deliberately held in reserve for wartime or emergency use and seldom, if ever, applied or intercepted prior to such use. Also called WARM.

APPENDIX D

References

United States Signal Intelligence Directives (USSIDs)

200   Technical SIGINT Reporting

340   Tactical ELINT Reporting

341   Technical ELINT Reporting

Allied Joint Publiction (AJP)

3.6   Allied Joint Electronic Warfare Doctrine

Military Committee (MC)

64   NATO EW Policy

298   Mutual SIGINT Support Between National and/or Multinational Tactical Formations Within NATO

422   NATO Policy for Information Operations

North Atlantic Treaty Organization (NATO) Standardization Agreement (STANAG)

5048   The Minimum Scale of Communications and Information Systems for NATO Land Forces

Joint Publications (JPs)

1-02   Department of Defense Dictionary of Military and Associated Terms

2-0   Doctrine for Intelligence Support to Joint Operations

3-0   Doctrine for Joint Operations

3-01.4   Joint Tactics, Techniques, and Procedures for Joint Suppression of Enemy Air Defenses (J-SEAD)

3-02   Joint Doctrine for Amphibious Operations

3-05.5   Joint Special Operations Targeting and Mission
              Planning Procedures

3-13   Joint Doctrine for Information Operations

3-51   Joint Doctrine for Electronic Warfare

3-54   Joint Doctrine for Operations Security

5-00.2   Joint Task Force (JTF) Planning Guidance and Procedures

Chairman of the Joint Chiefs of Staff Instructions (CJCSIs)

3320.01   Electromagnetic Spectrum Use in Joint Military Operations

3320.02   Spectrum Interference Resolution (JSIR)

6510.01   Information Assurance and Computer Network Defense

Chairman of the Joint Chiefs of Staff Manuals (CJCSMs)

3122.03   Joint Operation Planning and Execution System, Volume II,
              Planning Formats and Guidance

3320.1   Joint Operations in the Electromagnetic Battlespace

Office of the Chief of Naval Operations Instruction (OPNAVINST)

3430.23   Tactical Electronic Warfare Reprogrammable Library
              (EWRL) Support Program

Marine Corps Warfighting Publications (MCWPs)

2-1   Intelligence Operations

2-15.2   Signals Intelligence

www.ingramcontent.com/pod-product-compliance
Lightning Source LLC
Chambersburg PA
CBHW070602290526
45790CB00002B/748